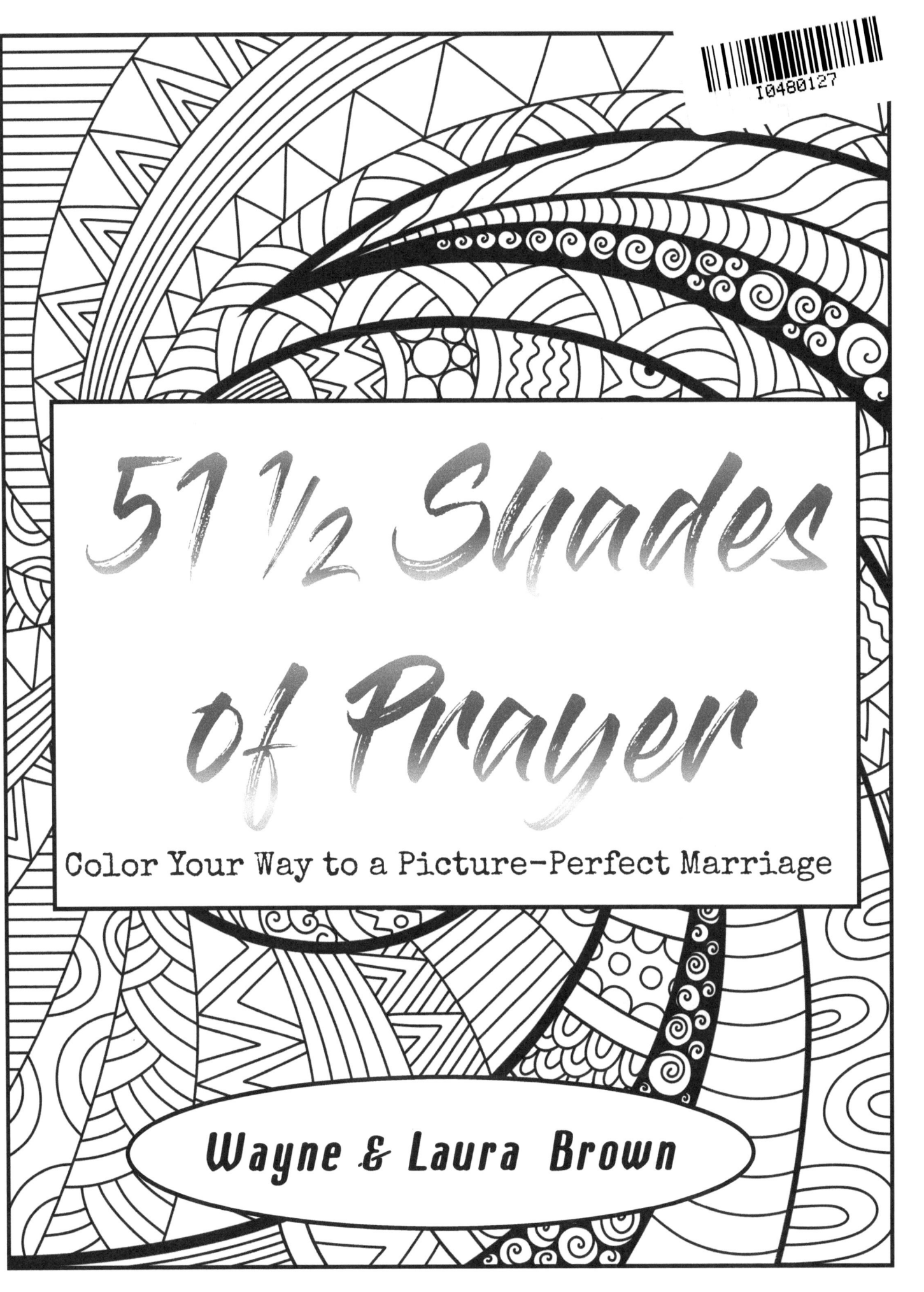

51 ½ Shades of Prayer

Color Your Way to a Picture-Perfect Marriage

Wayne & Laura Brown

Unless indicated otherwise, all scripture is from the King James Version

Printed in the United States of America

First Printing, 2018

ISBN 978-1-941749-82-1

4-P Publishing
Chattanooga, TN 37411

www.coachlaurabrown.com

Special Note

The *51 1/2 Shades of Prayer* Coloring Book is designed to be a companion to *51 1/2 Shades of Brown—The Not-So-Perfect Tales of a Picture-Perfect Marriage* book. Each picture has a "shade" - lesson learned from a story in the book. While you can certainly find some enjoyment from coloring and praying the scriptures, you will miss a vital piece of understanding the included "shade" without reading the story first.

If you do not have a copy of *51 1/2 Shades of Brown,* we recommend you head over to Amazon.com purchase a copy before you begin using *51 1/2 Shades of Prayer*. Additional copies of *51 1/2 Shades of Prayer* are only available through direct purchase at www.coachlaurabrown.com.

HOW TO USE THIS BOOK

1. Read the corresponding story in 51 1/2 Shades of Brown book.
2. Color and meditate on the "shade" and the scripture.
3. Write your prayer for your marriage. We have included a prayer starter, but feel free to use your own. There is space on both sides of the page to write your prayer or any additional notes or scriptures that come to mind.
4. If you using this book with your spouse or a prayer group, share your pictures and your prayers and prayer for each other!

We pray you enjoy the Picture-Perfect Marriage Coloring Experience!

Wayne & Laura

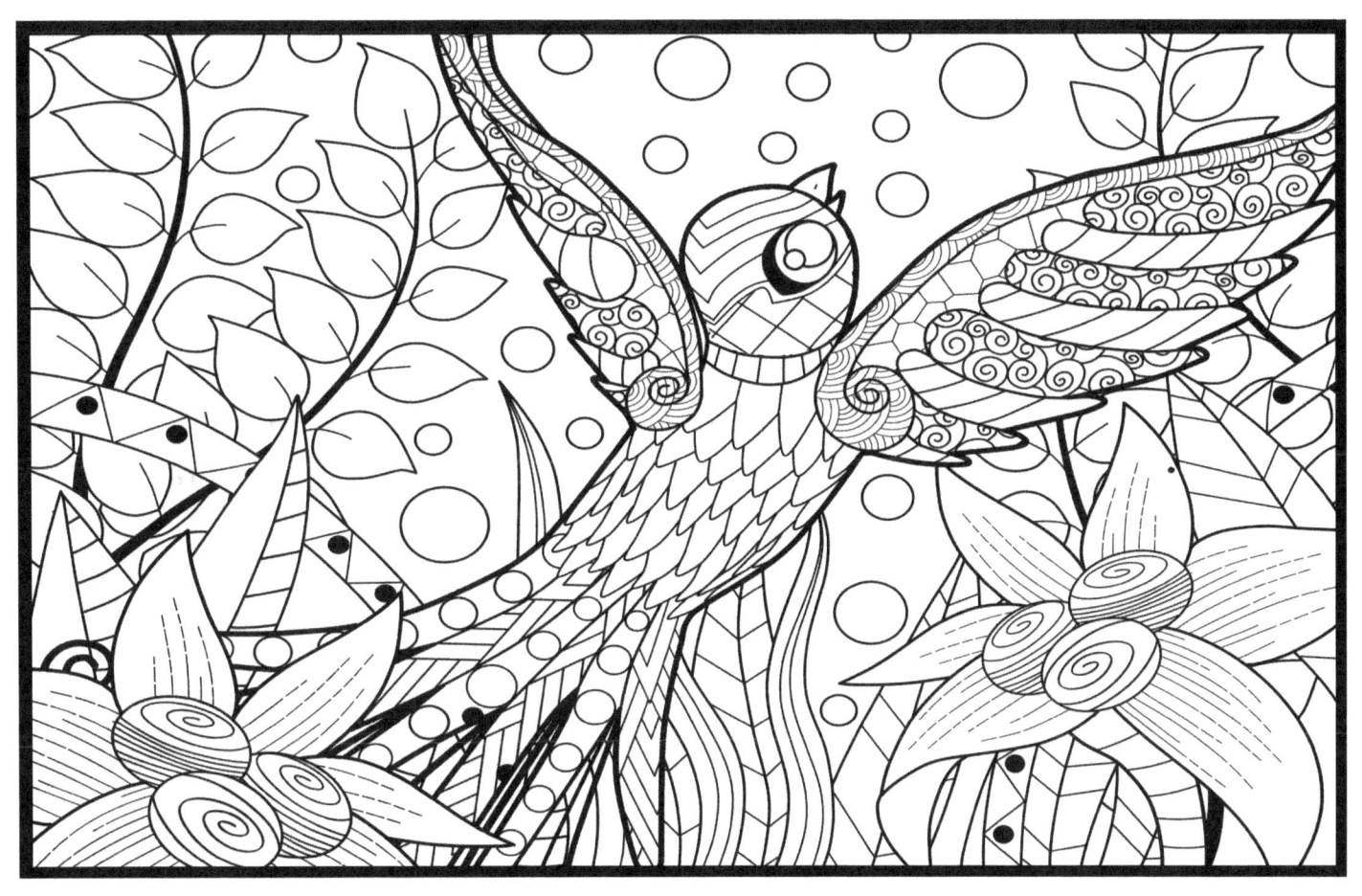

1. Embrace and value your authentic self.

Psalm 139:14

Lord, help us to color our marriage with...

I will praise thee; for I am fearfully *and* wonderfully made:
marvelous *are* thy works; and *that* my soul knoweth right well.
Psalm 139:14

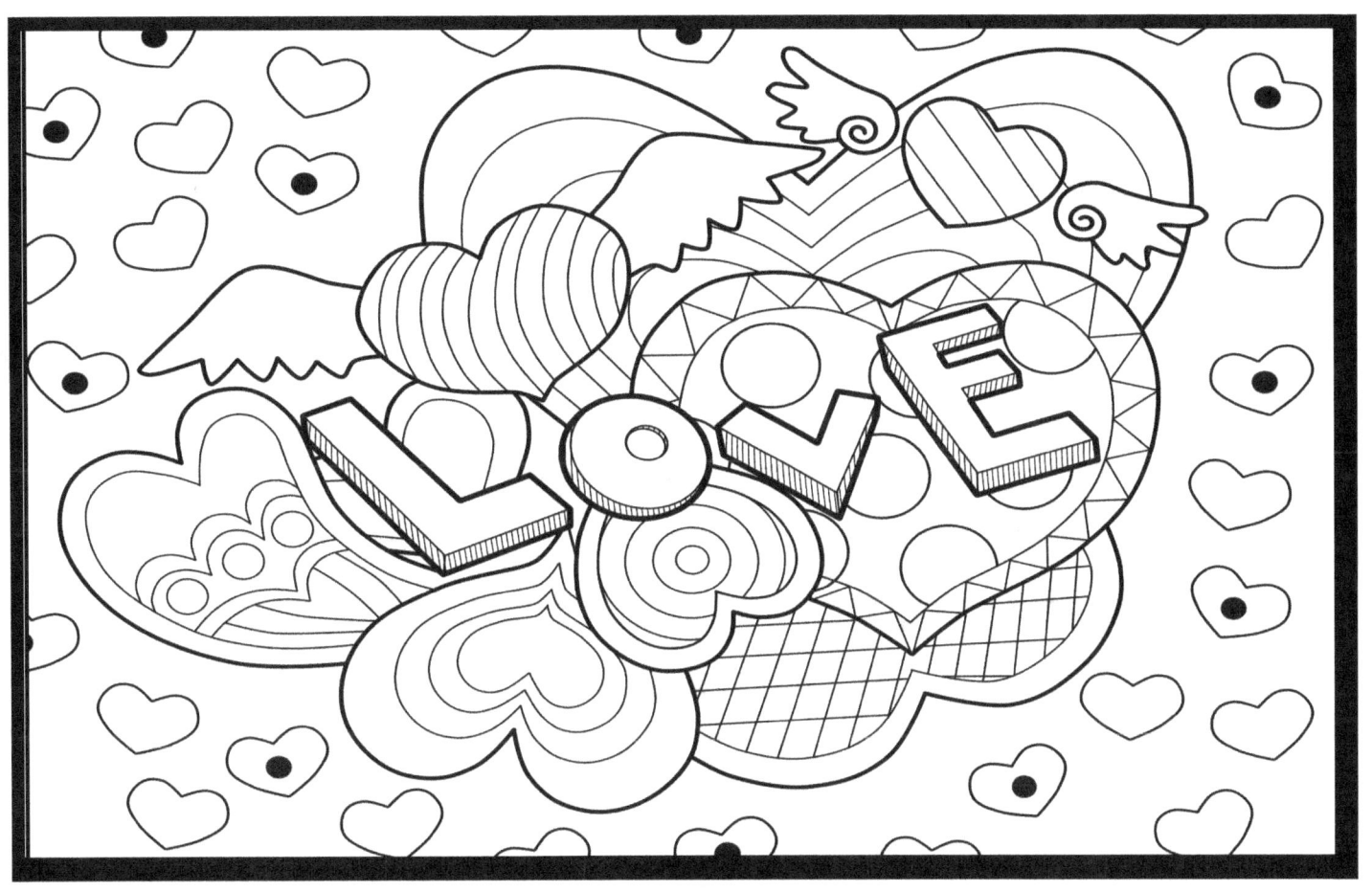

2. Silence your inner critic and engage in honest
communication with your spouse.

Ephesians 4:22-25

Lord, help us to color our marriage with...

That ye put off concerning the former conversation the old
man, which is corrupt according to the deceitful lusts;
And be renewed in the spirit of your mind;
And that ye put on the new man, which after God is created in
righteousness and true holiness.
Wherefore putting away lying, speak every man truth with his
neighbor: for we are members one of another.
Ephesians 4:22-25

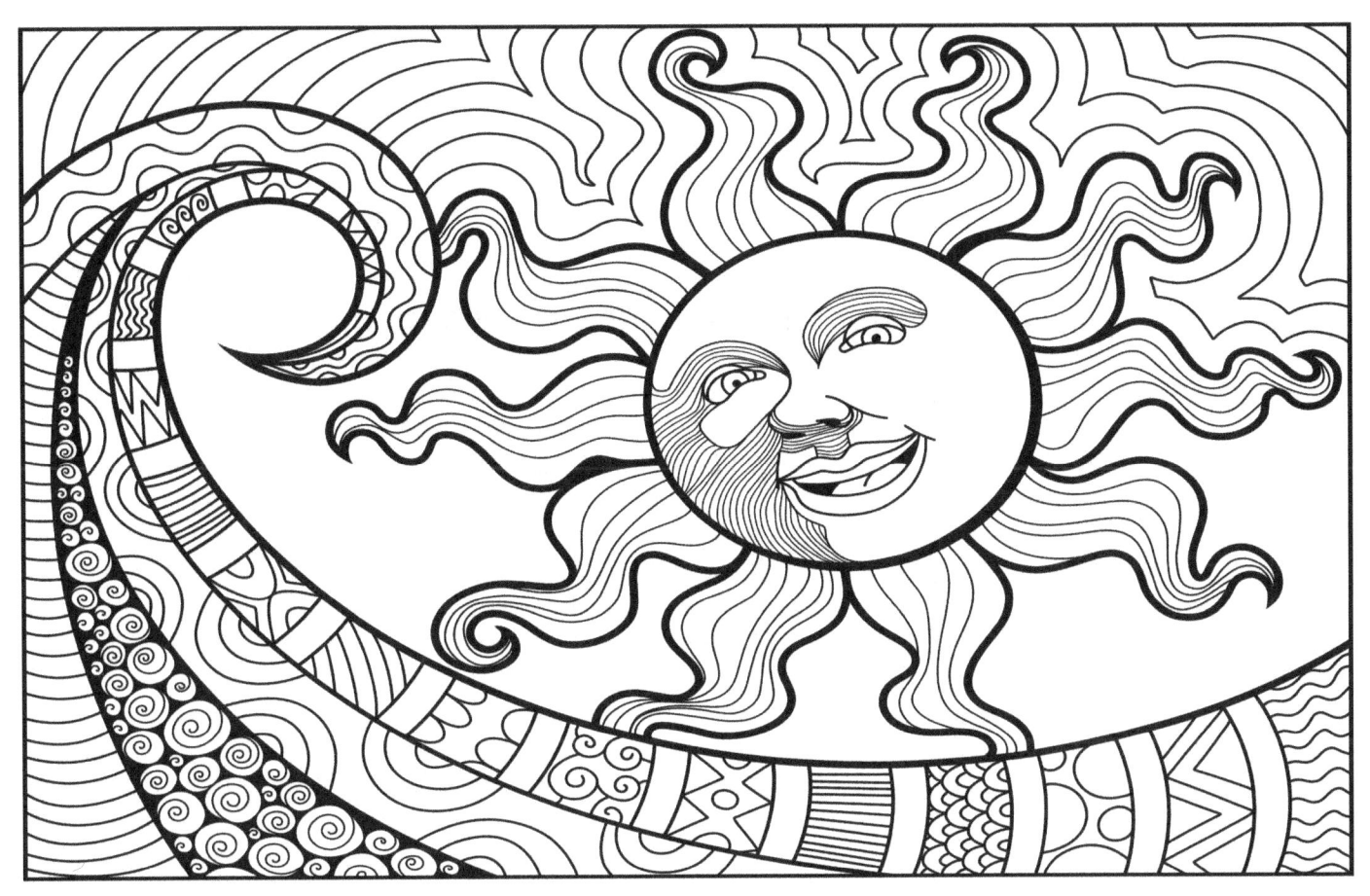

3. Learn to laugh at yourself.

Proverbs 17:22

Lord, help us to color our marriage with…

A merry heart doeth good like a medicine:
but a broken spirit drieth the bones.
Proverbs 17:22

_____
_____
_____
_____
_____
_____
_____
_____
_____
_____
_____

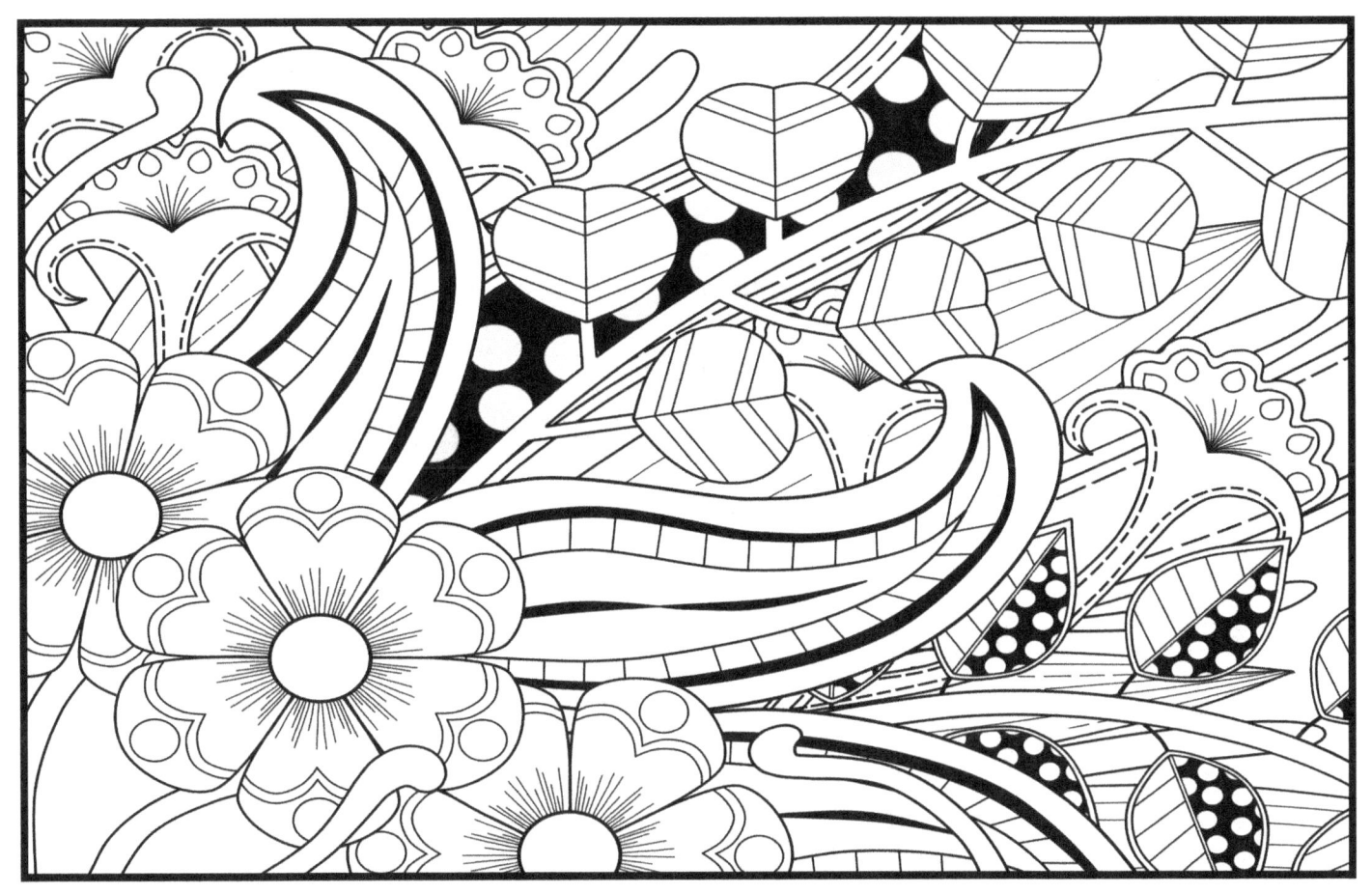

4. Stay untangled from deceit.

Psalm 32:1-2

Lord, help us to color our marriage with…

Blessed is he whose transgression is forgiven,

whose sin is covered.

Blessed is the man unto whom the Lord imputeth not iniquity,

and in whose spirit there is no guile.

Psalm 32:1-2

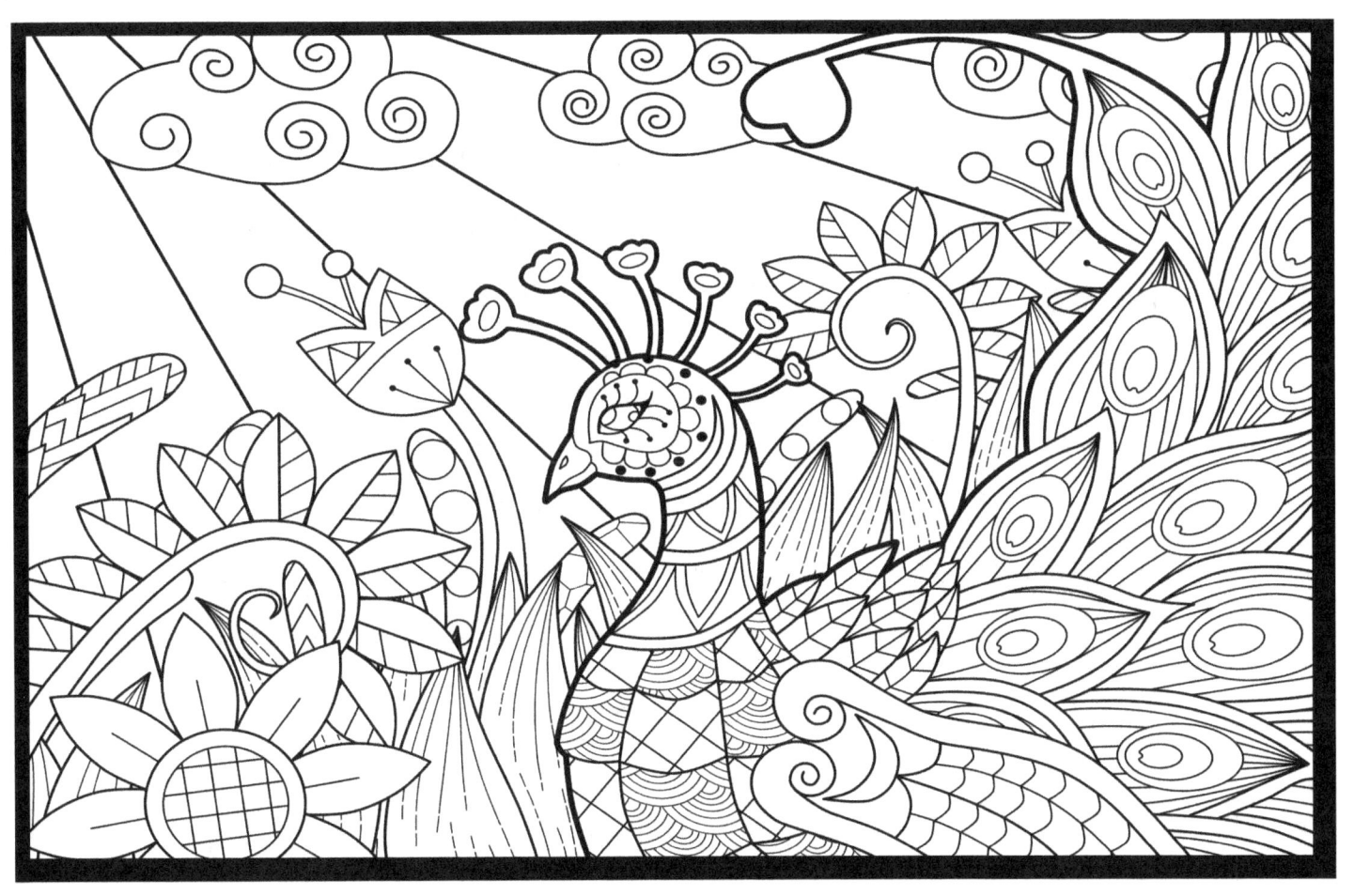

5. Lead with confidence versus ego.

Philippians 2:1-5

Lord, help us to color our marriage with...

_____

_____

_____

_____

_____

_____

_____

_____

_____

_____

If there be therefore any consolation in Christ, if any comfort of love, if any fellowship of the Spirit, if any bowels and mercies, fulfil ye my joy, that ye be likeminded, having the same love, being of one accord, of one mind. Let nothing be done through strife or vainglory; but in lowliness of mind let each esteem other better than themselves. Look not every man on his own things, but every man also on the things of others. Let this mind be in you, which was also in Christ Jesus...

Philippians 2:1-5

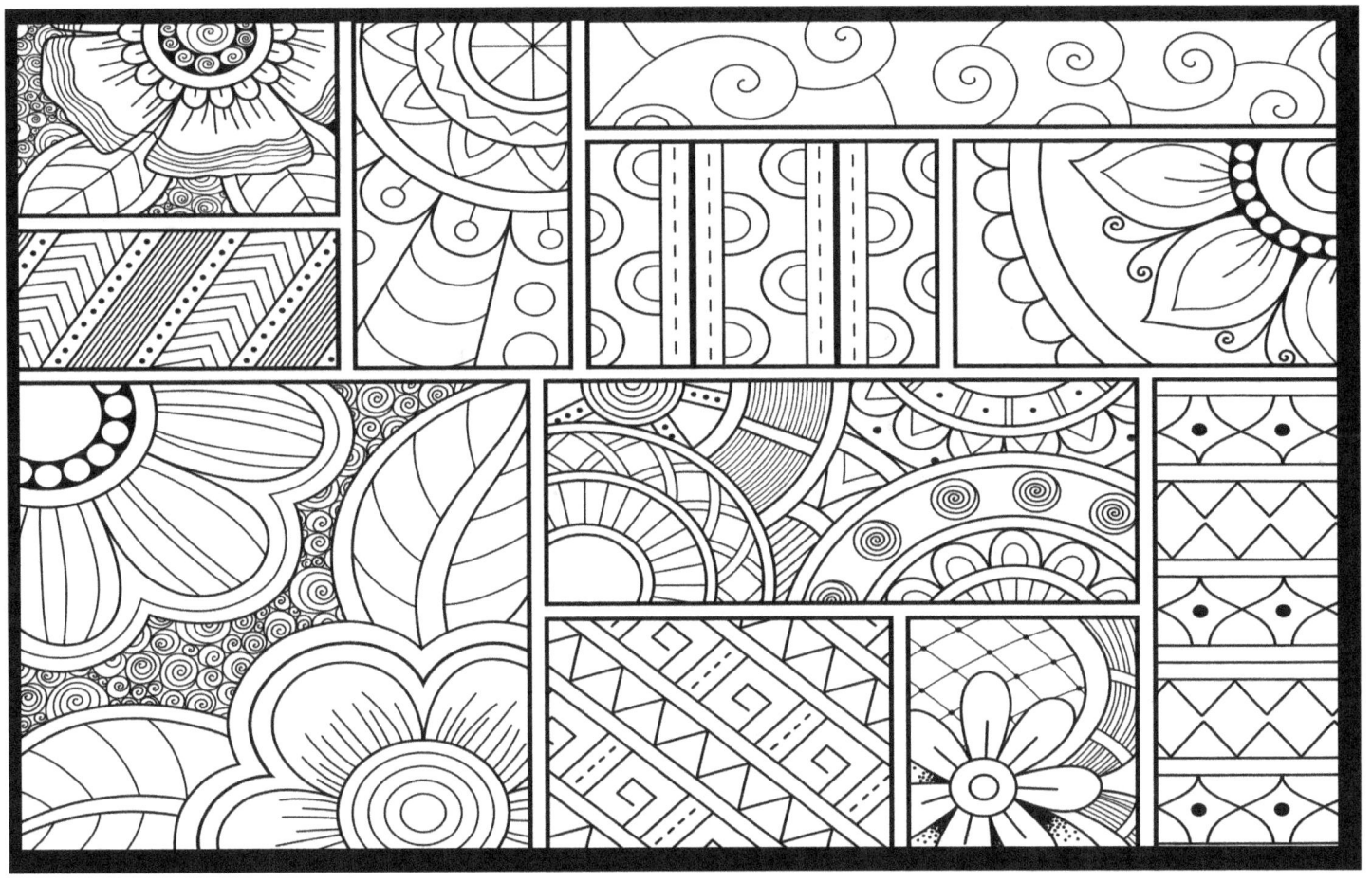

6. Focus on hidden treasures.

Matthew 13:44

Lord, help us to color our marriage with...

_____

_____

_____

_____

_____

_____

_____

_____

_____

_____

_____

Again, the kingdom of heaven is like unto treasure hid in a field; the which when a man hath found, he hideth, and for joy thereof goeth and selleth all that he hath, and buyeth that field.

Matthew 13:44

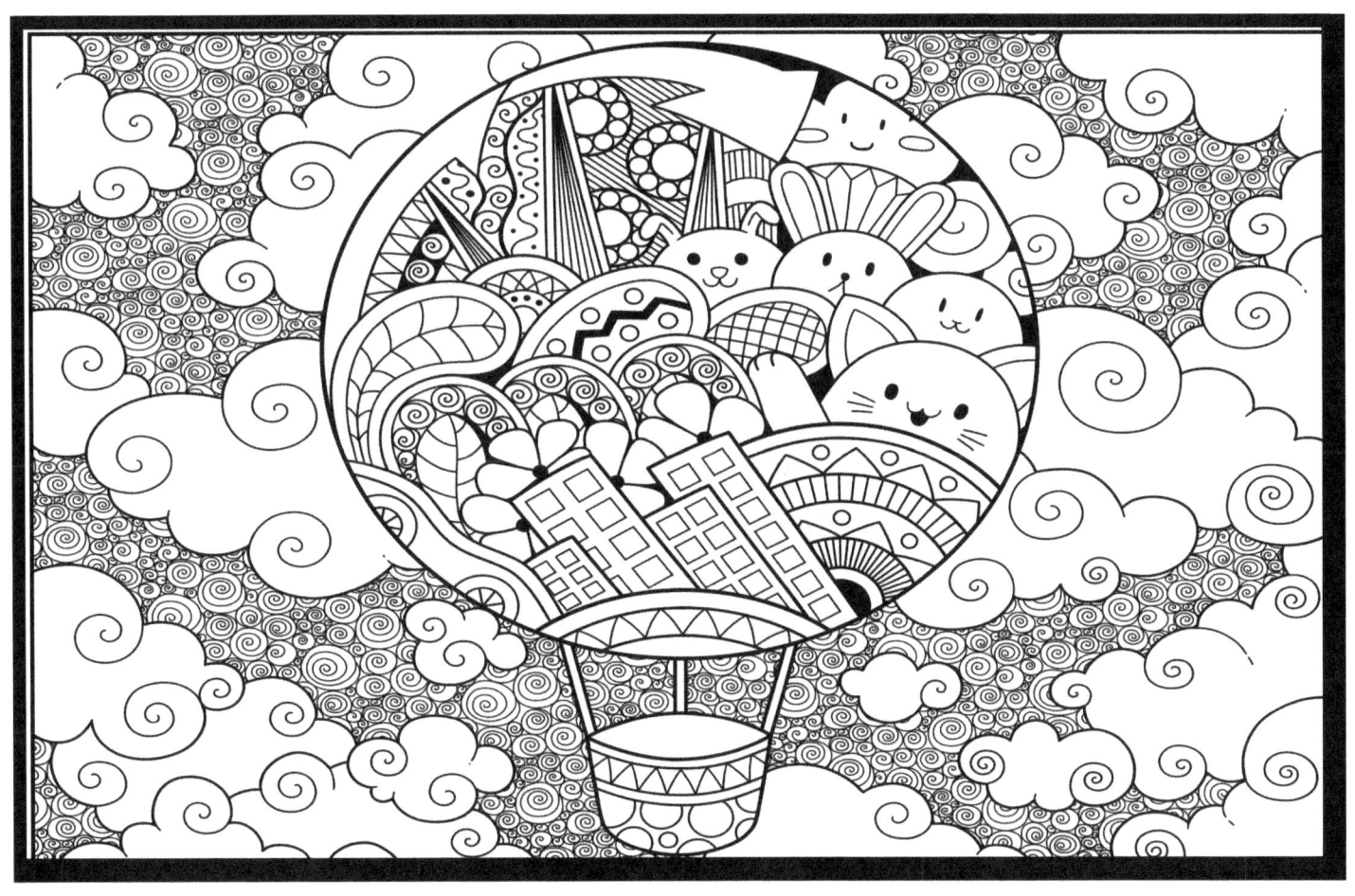

7. Learn to let go of some things.

I Corinthians 13:11

Lord, help us to color our marriage with…

_____

_____

_____

_____

_____

_____

_____

_____

_____

_____

_____

When I was a child, I spake as a child, I understood as a child,
I thought as a child: but when I became a man,
I put away childish things.
I Corinthians 13:11

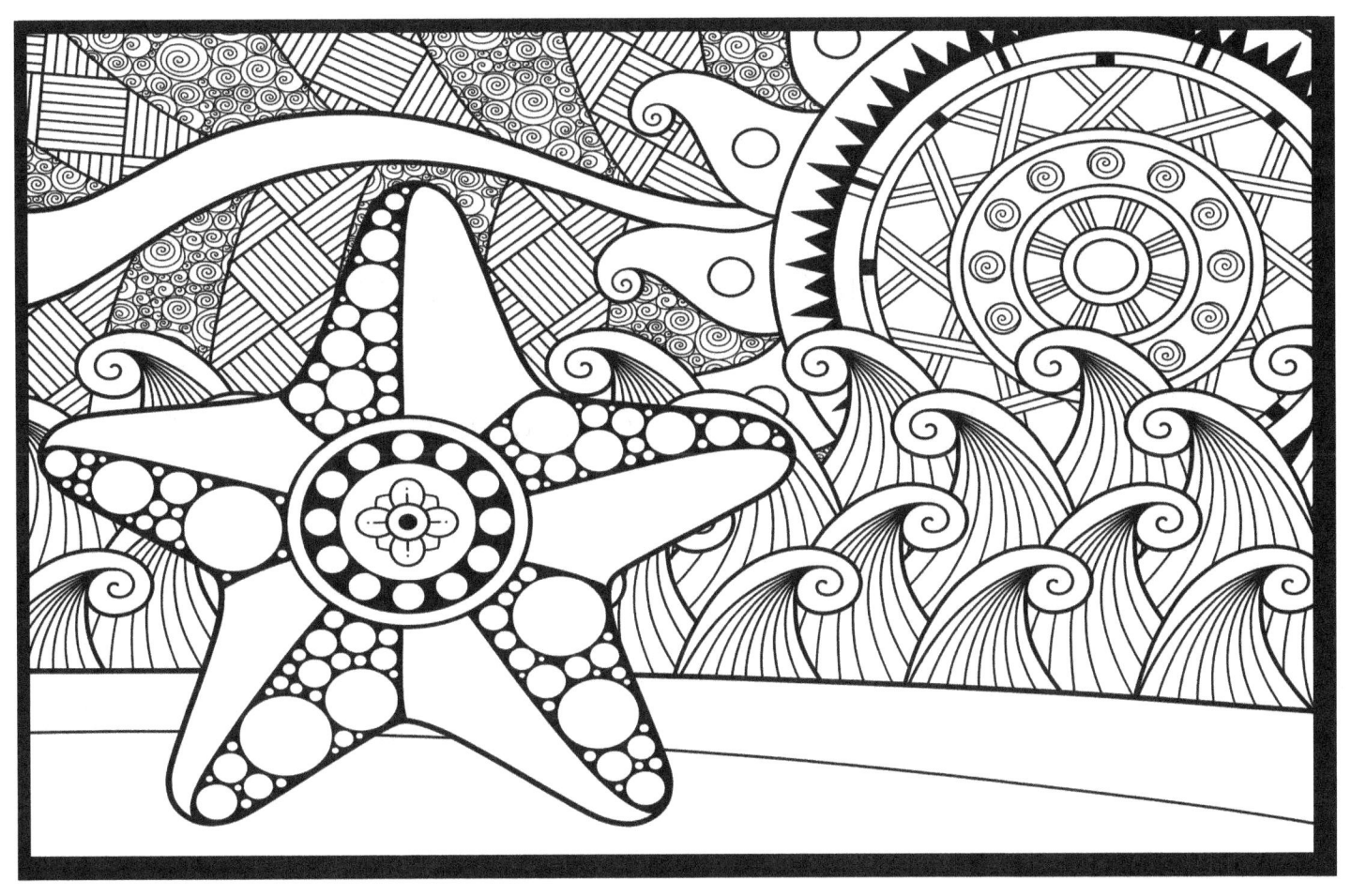

8. Learn to recognize the signs of unchecked baggage.

Psalm 139:23-24

Lord, help us to color our marriage with...

_____

_____

_____

_____

_____

_____

_____

_____

_____

_____

_____

_____

Search me, O God, and know my heart:
try me, and know my thoughts:
and see if there be any wicked way in me,
and lead me in the way everlasting.
Psalm 139:23-24

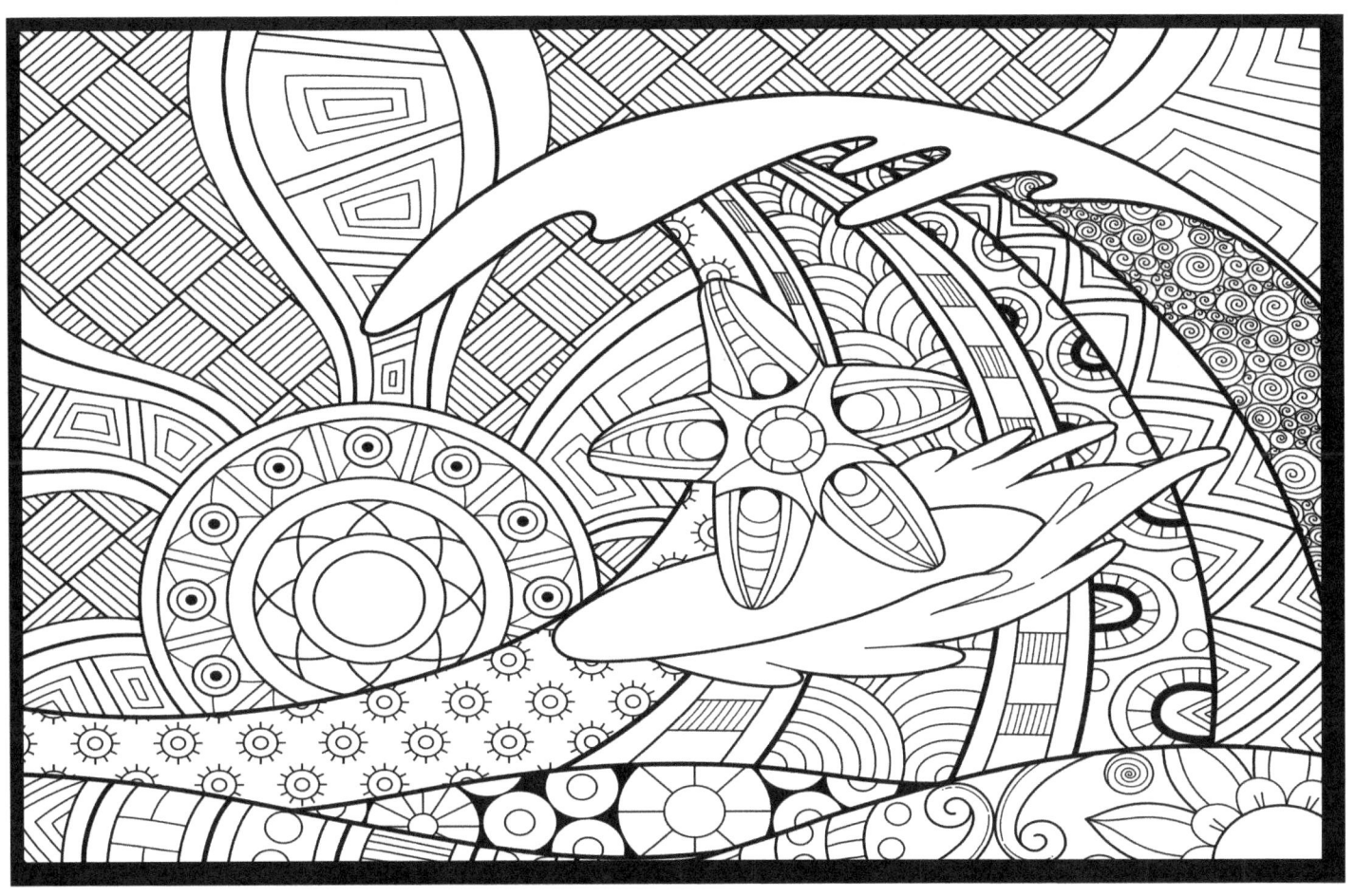

9. Do not let low self-worth cause you to project

your fears and worries onto your spouse.

Luke 12:6-7

Lord, help us to color our marriage with...

Are not five sparrows sold for two farthings, and not one of them is forgotten before God? But even the very hairs of your head are all numbered. Fear not therefore: ye are of more value than many sparrows.

Luke 12:6-7

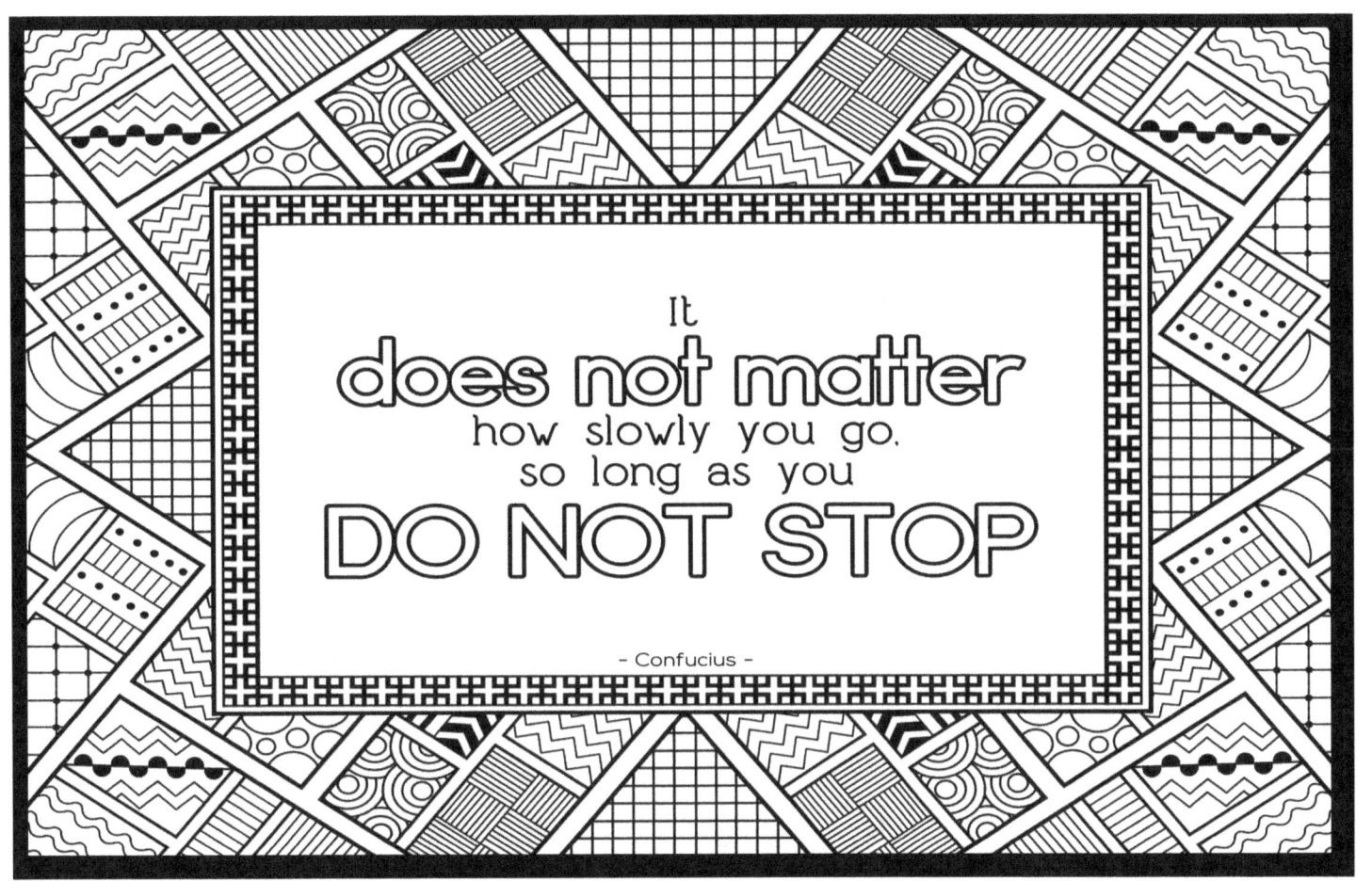

It
does not matter
how slowly you go,
so long as you
DO NOT STOP

- Confucius -

10. Make a decision to move forward and don't look back.

Philippians 3:13-14; Isaiah 43:18-19

Lord, help us to color our marriage with...

Brethren, I count not myself to have apprehended: but this one thing I do, forgetting those things which are behind, and reaching forth unto those things which are before. I press toward the mark for the prize of the high calling of God in Christ Jesus.

Philippians 3:13-14

Remember ye not the former things, neither consider the things of old. Behold, I will do a new thing; now it shall spring forth; shall ye not know it?

Isaiah 43:18-19

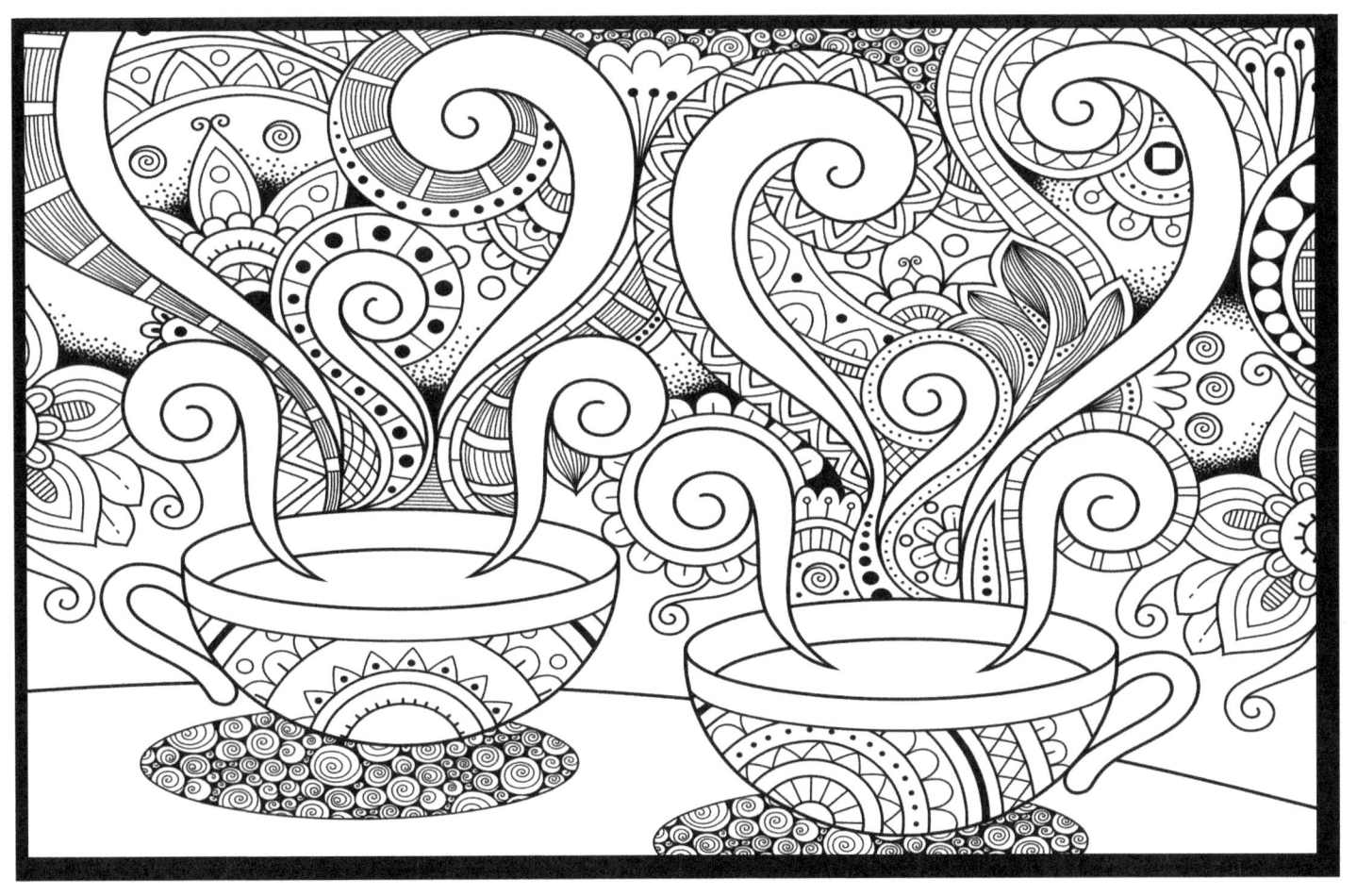

11. Find joy in moments that go awry.

Philippians 4:4

Lord, help us to color our marriage with...
_____
_____
_____
_____
_____
_____
_____
_____
_____
_____
_____

Rejoice in the Lord always: and again I say, Rejoice. Let your moderation be known unto all men. The Lord is at hand.

Philippians 4:4-5

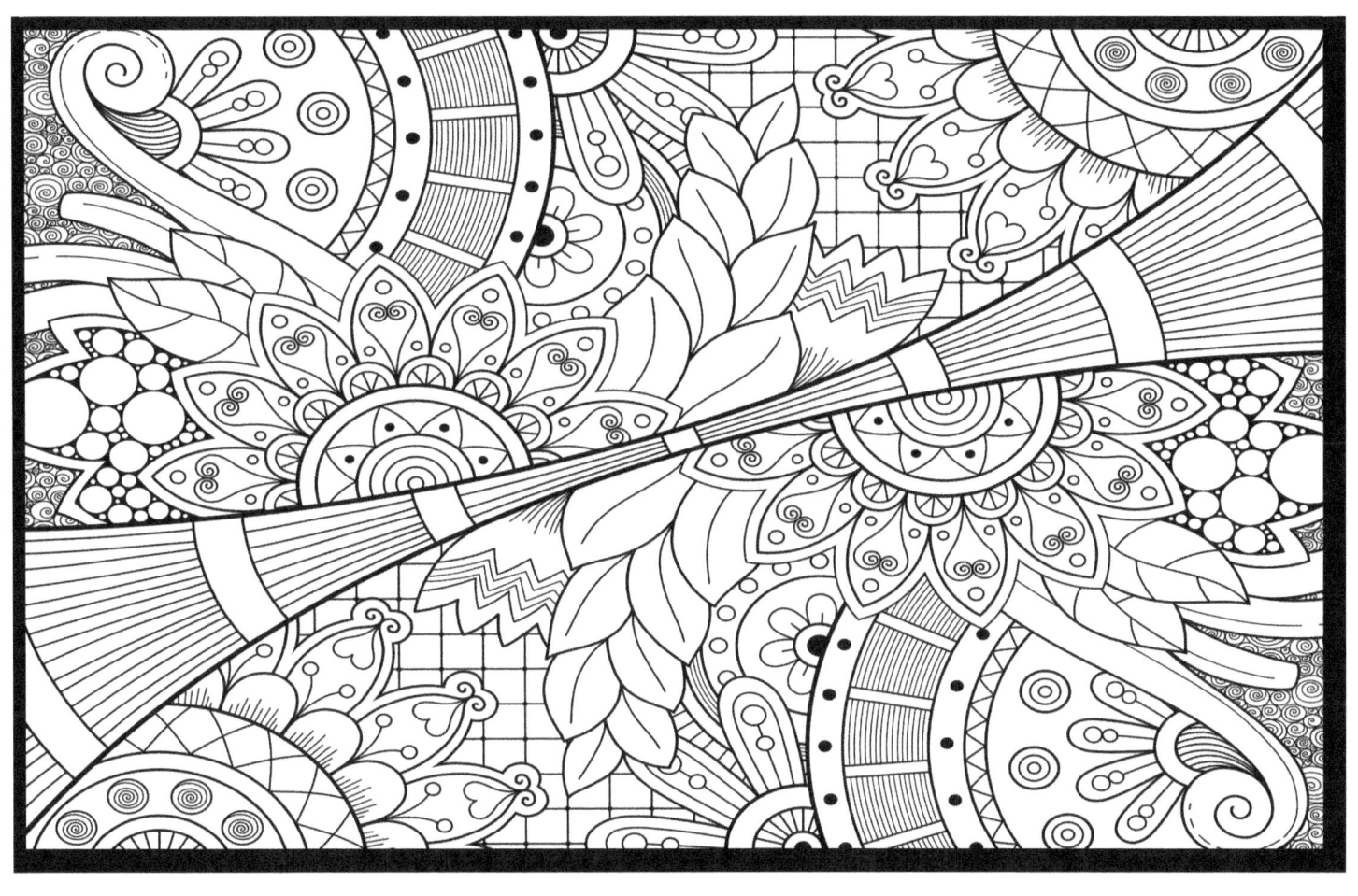

12. Learn the best way to encourage your spouse.

Proverbs 27:17

Lord, help us to color our marriage with...

_____
_____
_____
_____
_____
_____
_____
_____
_____
_____
_____

Iron sharpeneth iron;

so a man sharpeneth the countenance of his friend.

Proverbs 27:17

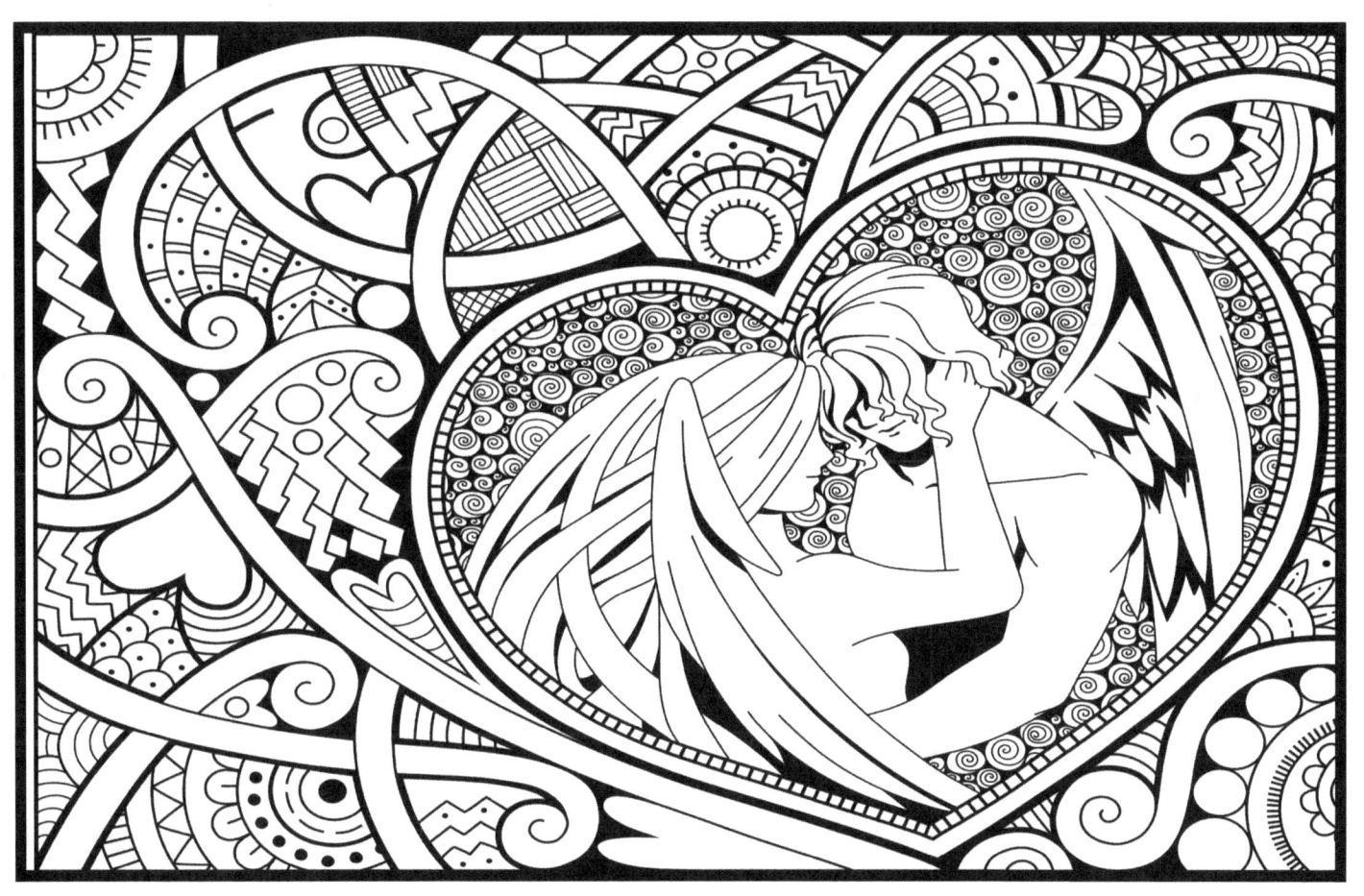

13. Always protect each other.

John 15:12-13

Lord, help us to color our marriage with...

_____
_____
_____
_____
_____
_____
_____
_____
_____
_____
_____

This is my commandment, That ye love one another, as I have
loved you. Greater love hath no man than this, that a man lay
down his life for his friends.

John 15:12-13

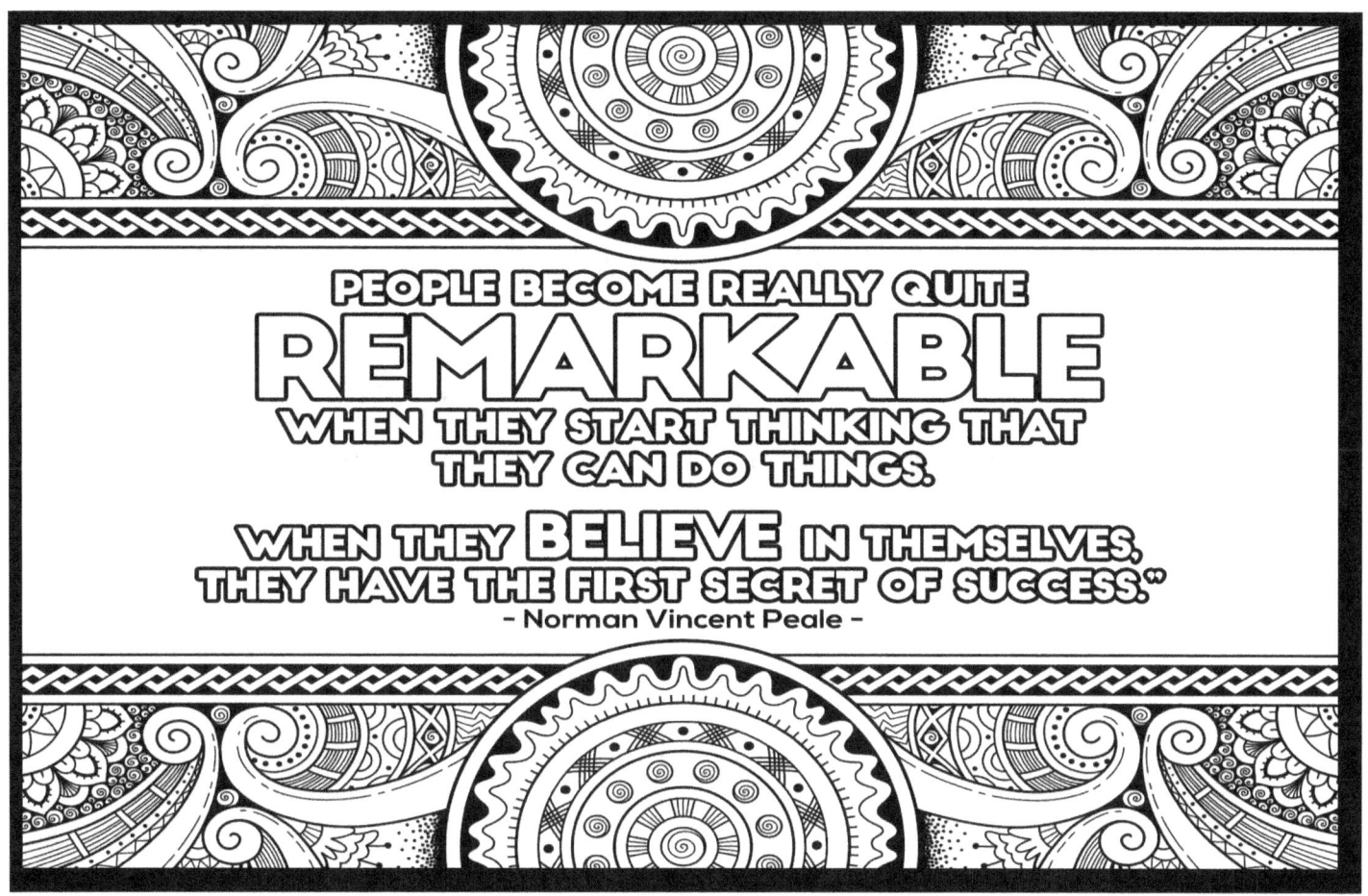

PEOPLE BECOME REALLY QUITE
REMARKABLE
WHEN THEY START THINKING THAT
THEY CAN DO THINGS.

WHEN THEY BELIEVE IN THEMSELVES,
THEY HAVE THE FIRST SECRET OF SUCCESS."
- Norman Vincent Peale -

14. Don't miss opportune moments waiting for the perfect time.

John 2:1-5

Lord, help us to color our marriage with...

And the third day there was a marriage in Cana of Galilee; and the mother of Jesus was there: and both Jesus was called, and his disciples, to the marriage. And when they wanted wine, the mother of Jesus saith unto him, They have no wine. Jesus saith unto her, Woman, what have I to do with thee? mine hour is not yet come. His mother saith unto the servants, Whatsoever he saith unto you, do it...This beginning of miracles did Jesus in Cana of Galilee, and manifested forth his glory; and his disciples believed on him.

John 2:1-5, 11

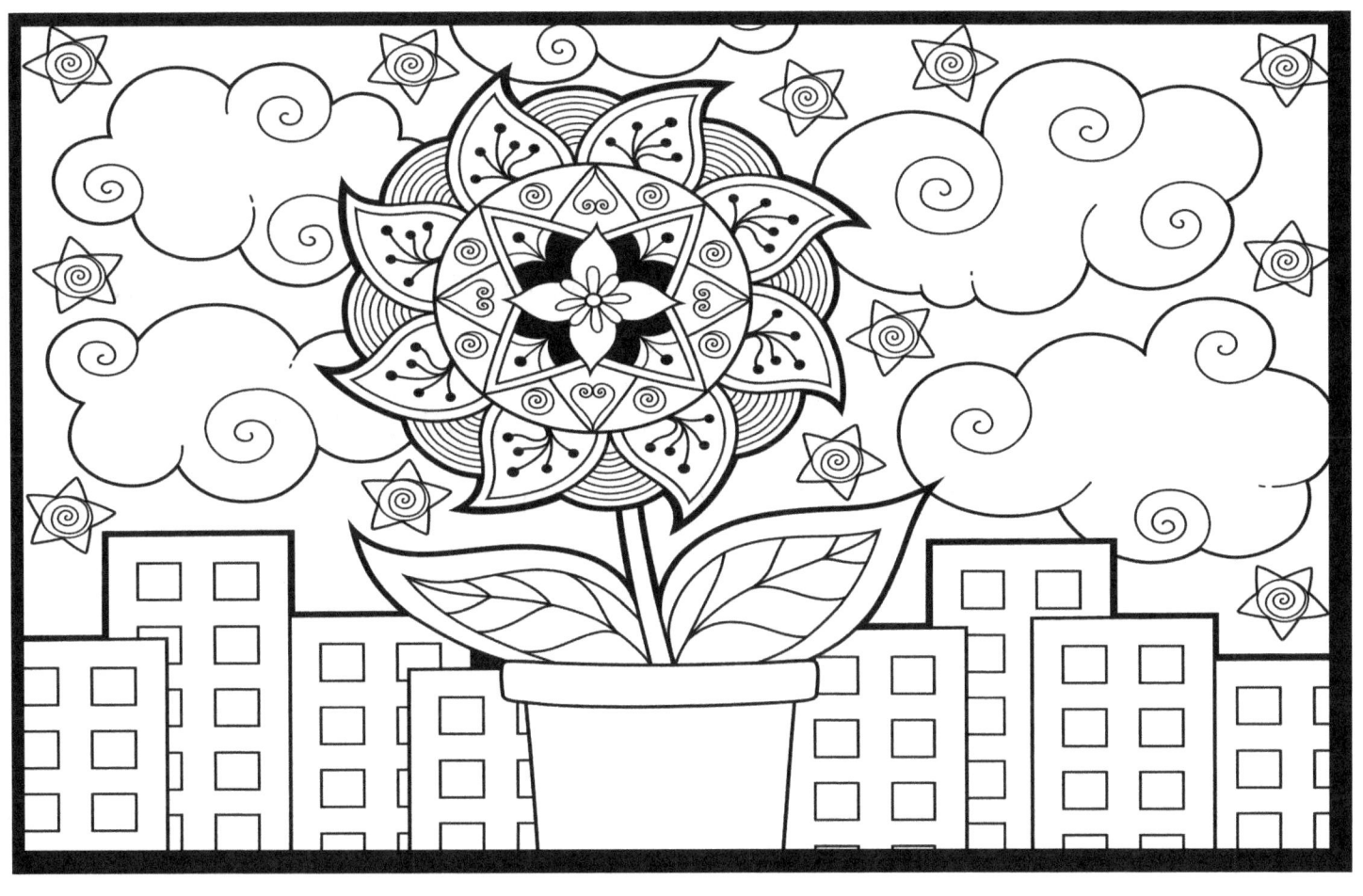

15. Learn the art of sacrifice.

Philippians 2:3-5

Lord, help us to color our marriage with...

_____

_____

_____

_____

_____

_____

_____

_____

_____

_____

_____

Let nothing be done through strife or vainglory; but in lowliness of mind let each esteem other better than themselves. Look not every man on his own things, but every man also on the things of others. Let this mind be in you, which was also in Christ Jesus...

Philippians 2:3-5

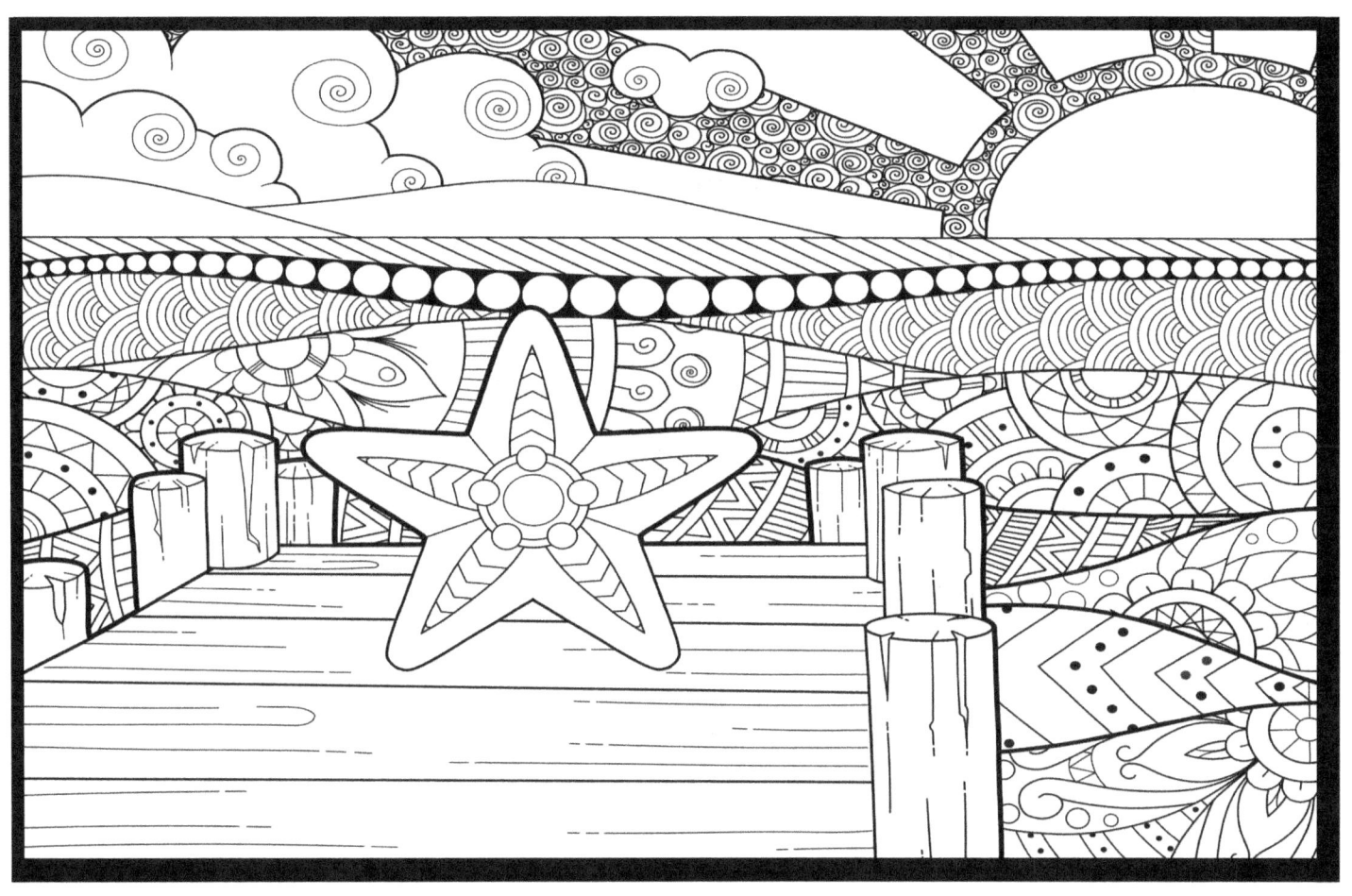

16. Be careful who you invite into your marriage.
Psalm 1:1-3; I Corinthians 15:33

Lord, help us to color our marriage with...

_____
_____
_____
_____
_____
_____
_____
_____
_____
_____
_____

Blessed is the man that walketh

not in the counsel of the ungodly,

nor standeth in the way of sinners,

nor sitteth in the seat of the scornful.

But his delight is in the law of the Lord;

and in his law doth he meditate day and night.

And he shall be like a tree planted by the rivers of water,

that bringeth forth his fruit in his season;

his leaf also shall not wither;

and whatsoever he doeth shall prosper.

Psalm 1:1-3

Be not deceived: evil communications corrupt good manners.

I Corinthians 15:33

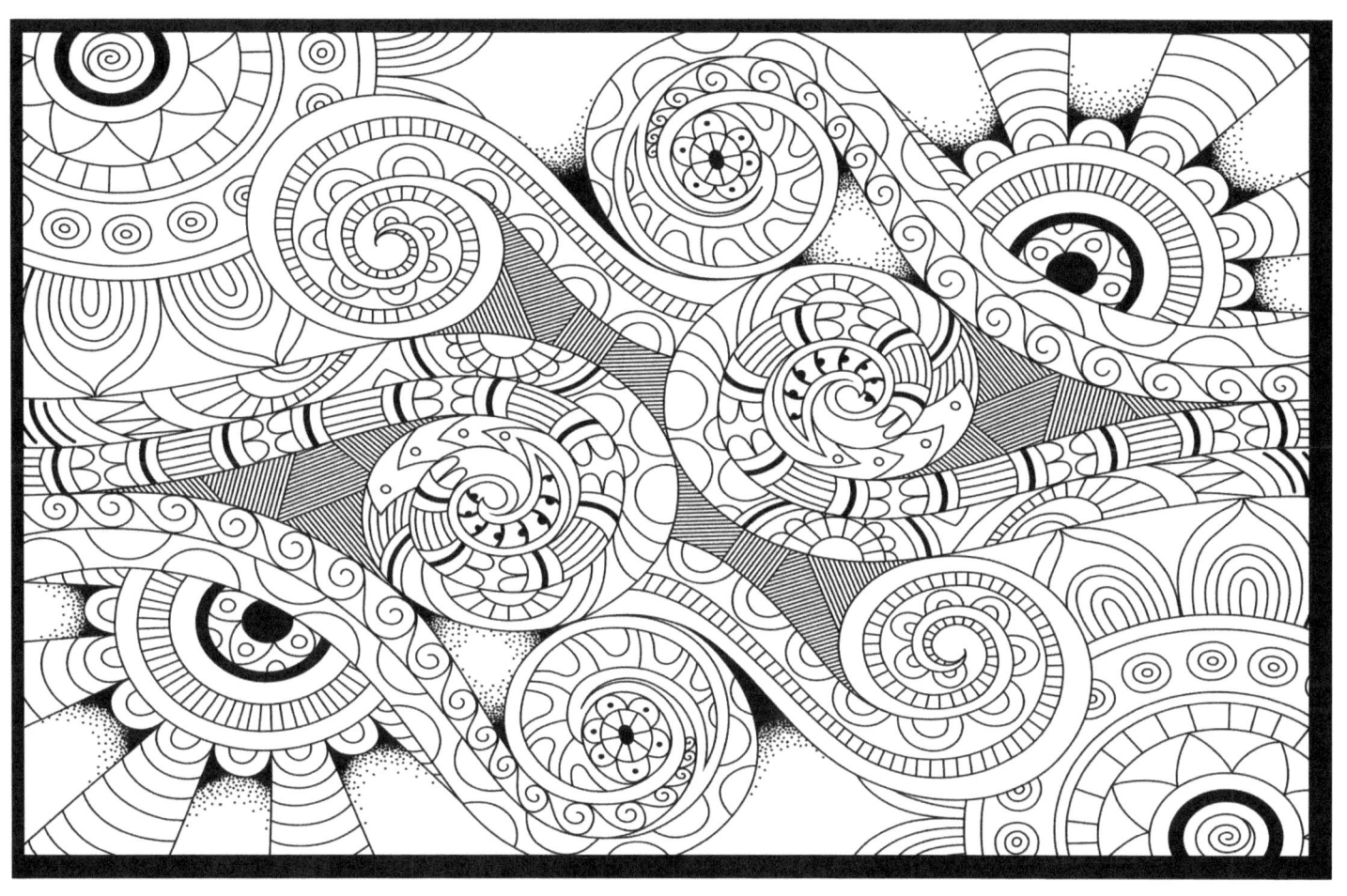

17. View your spouse with fresh eyes.

II Kings 6:17

Lord, help us to color our marriage with…

_____

_____

_____

_____

_____

_____

_____

_____

_____

_____

_____

And Elisha prayed, and said, Lord, I pray thee, open his eyes,
that he may see. And the Lord opened the eyes of the young
man; and he saw: and, behold, the mountain was full of horses
and chariots of fire round about Elisha

II Kings 6:17

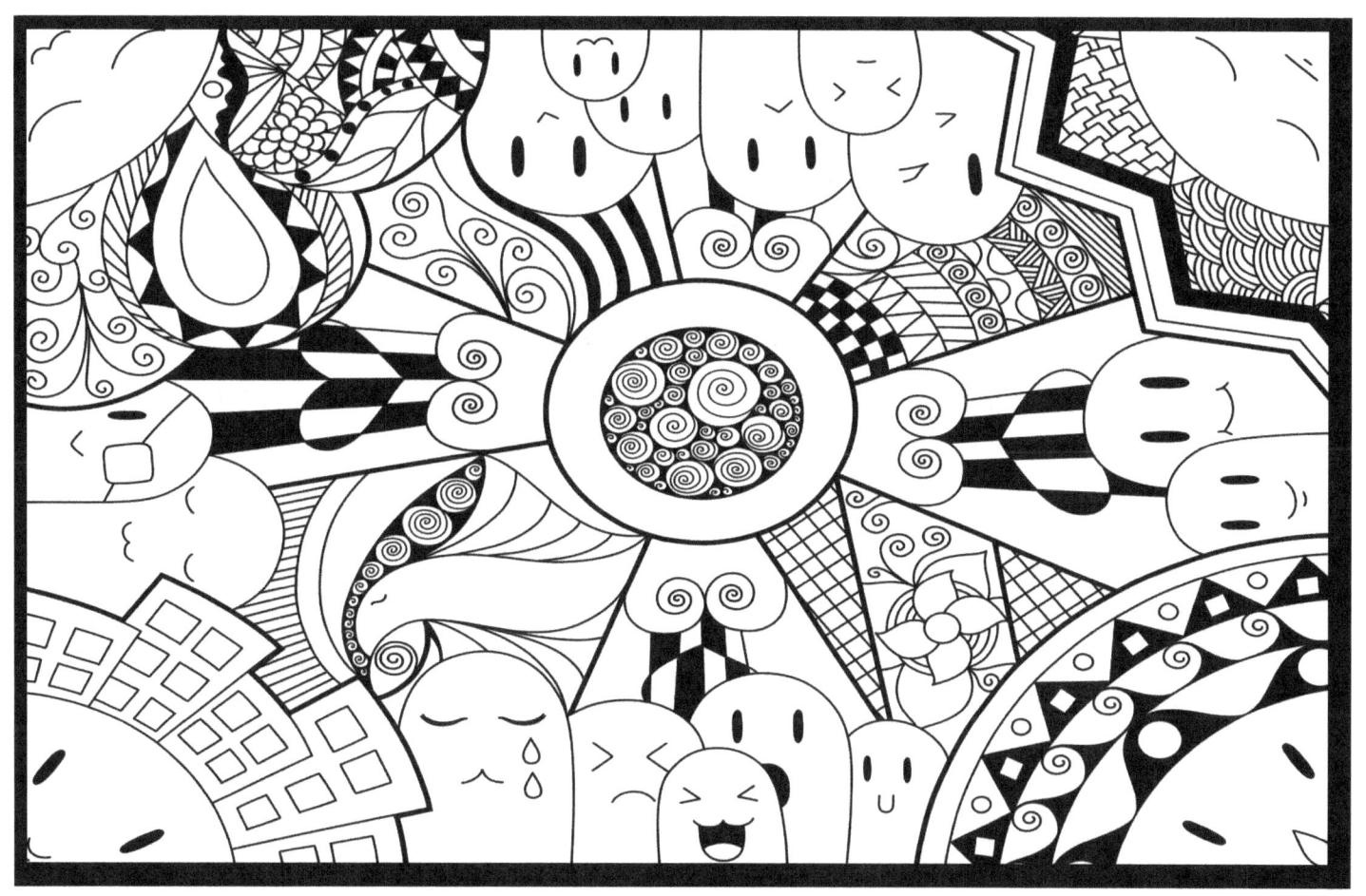

18. Have brave conversations.

John 4:7-26

Lord, help us to color our marriage with...

_____

_____

_____

_____

_____

_____

_____

_____

_____

_____

_____

_____

There cometh a woman of Samaria to draw water: Jesus saith unto her, Give me to drink. (For his disciples were gone away unto the city to buy meat.) Then saith the woman of Samaria unto him, How is it that thou, being a Jew, askest drink of me, which am a woman of Samaria? for the Jews have no dealings with the Samaritans. Jesus answered and said unto her, If thou knewest the gift of God, and who it is that saith to thee, Give me to drink; thou wouldest have asked of him, and he would have given thee living water...

Jesus saith unto her, Go, call thy husband, and come hither. The woman answered and said, I have no husband. Jesus said unto her, Thou hast well said, I have no husband: for thou hast had five husbands; and he whom thou now hast is not thy husband: in that saidst thou truly. The woman saith unto him, Sir, I perceive that thou art a prophet... The woman saith unto him, I know that Messiah cometh, which is called Christ: when he is come, he will tell us all things. Jesus saith unto her, I that speak unto thee am he.

John 4:7-26

(Please read the passage in its entirety)

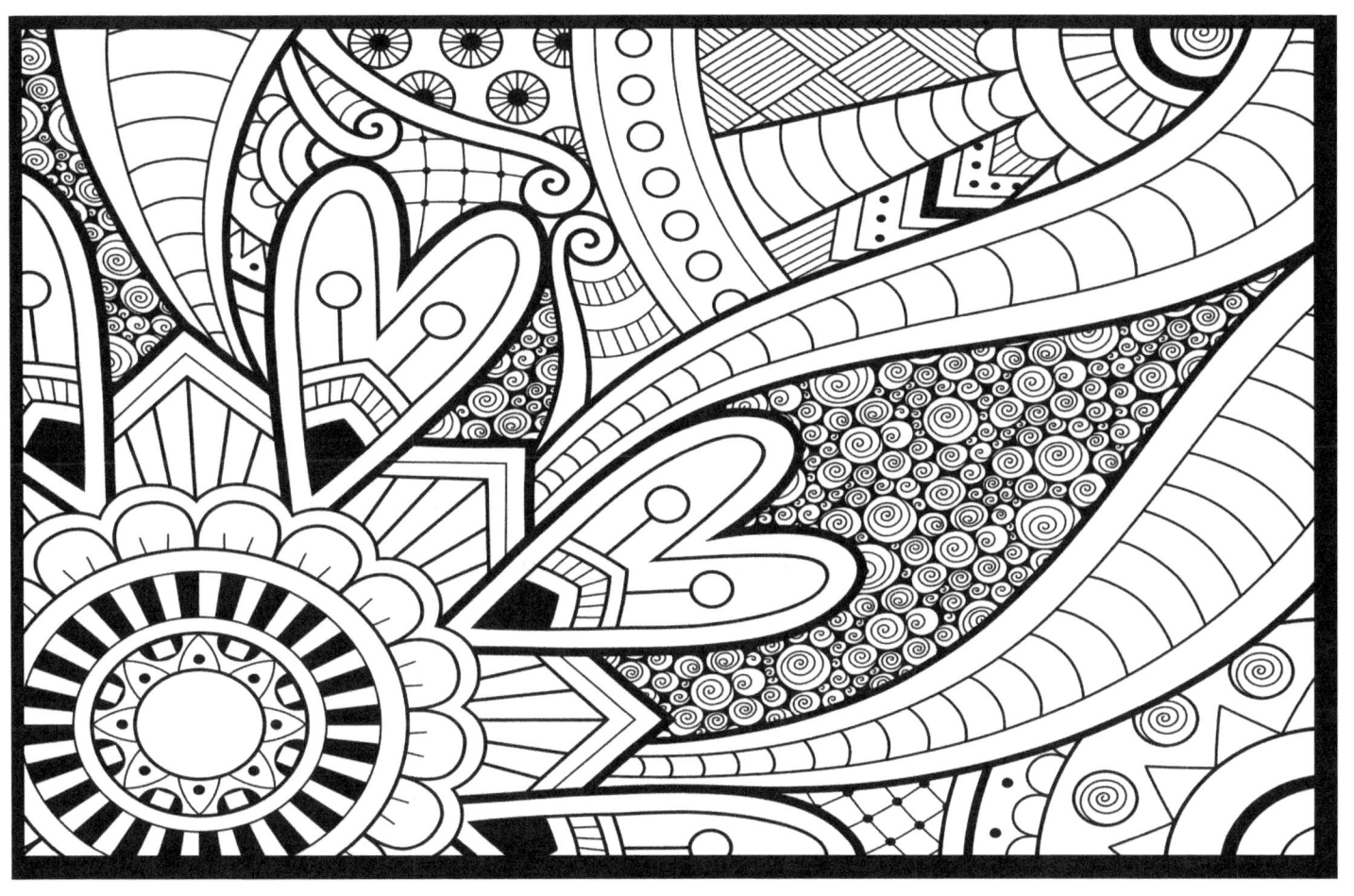

19. Practice silence and let God speak to your spouse.

Proverbs 17:27-28

Lord, help us to color our marriage with...

_____
_____
_____
_____
_____
_____
_____
_____
_____
_____
_____

He that hath knowledge spareth his words:

and a man of understanding is of an excellent spirit.

2Even a fool, when he holdeth his peace, is counted wise:

and he that shutteth his lips is esteemed a man of understanding.

Proverbs 17:27-28

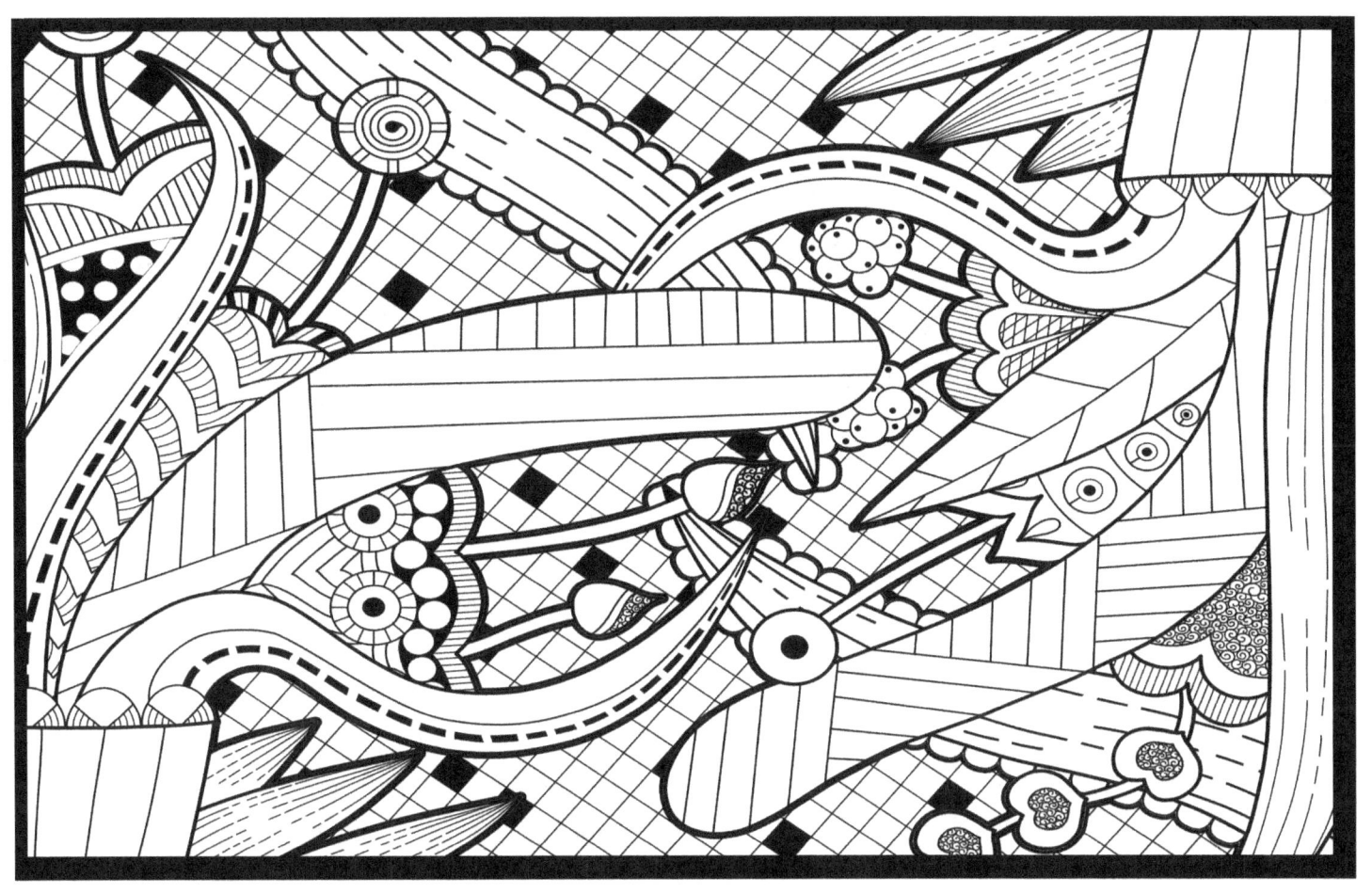

20. Learn to conquer sexual temptation.
I Corinthians 10:13-14

Lord, help us to color our marriage with...

_____
_____
_____
_____
_____
_____
_____
_____
_____
_____
_____

There hath no temptation taken you but such as is common to man: but God is faithful, who will not suffer you to be tempted above that ye are able; but will with the temptation also make a way to escape, that ye may be able to bear it. Wherefore, my dearly beloved, flee from idolatry.

I Corinthians 10:13-14

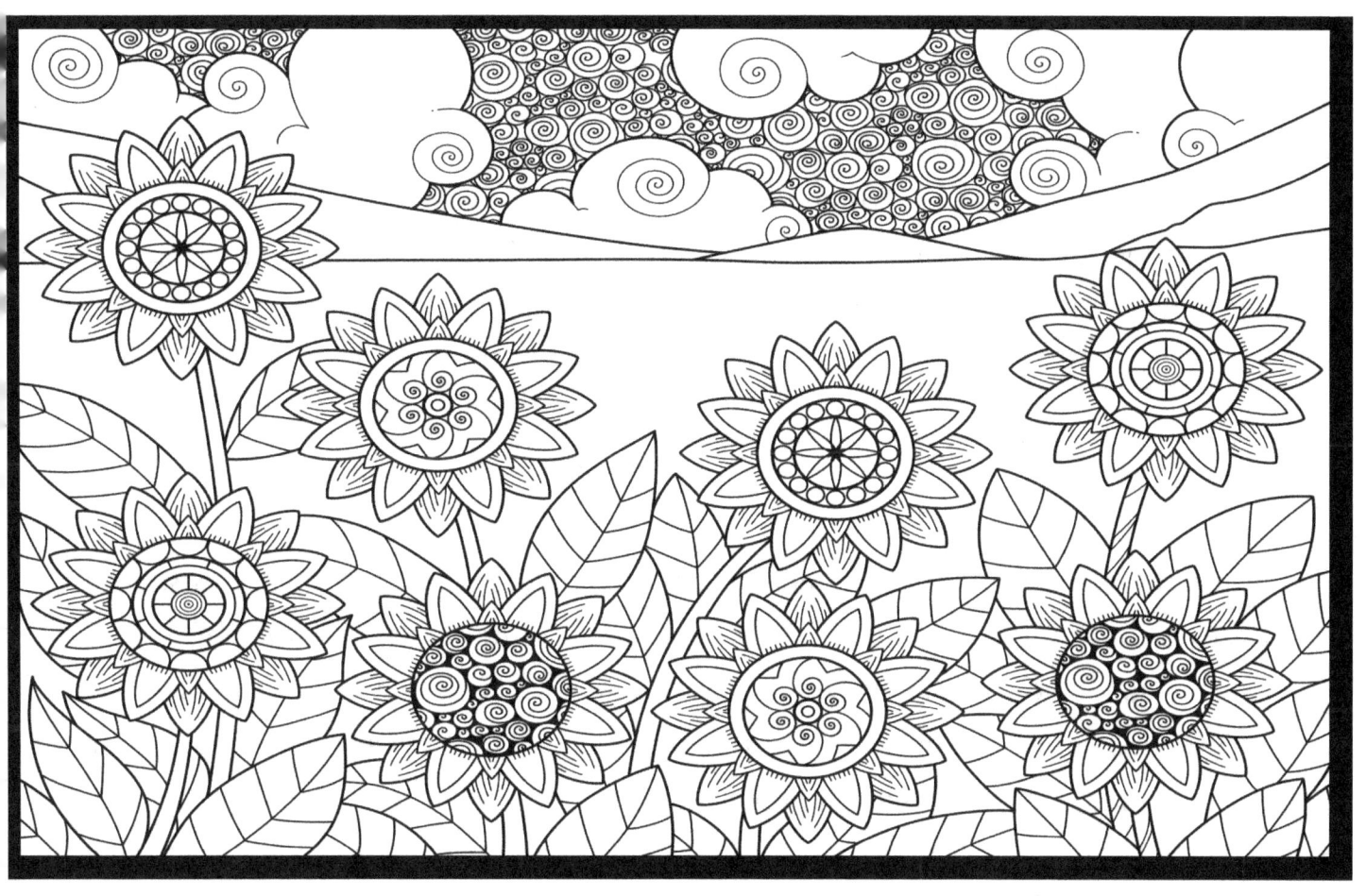

21. Be a source of pride and not embarrassment for your spouse.

Genesis 2:21-25

Lord, help us to color our marriage with...

And the Lord God caused a deep sleep to fall upon Adam, and he slept; and he took one of his ribs, and closed up the flesh instead thereof. And the rib, which the Lord God had taken from man, made he a woman, and brought her unto the man. And Adam said, This is now bone of my bones, and flesh of my flesh: she shall be called Woman. Therefore shall a man leave his father and his mother, and shall cleave unto his wife: and they shall be one flesh. And they were both naked, the man and his wife, and were not ashamed.

Genesis 2:21-25

And when the woman saw that the tree was good for food, and that it was pleasant to the eyes, and a tree to be desired to make one wise, she took of the fruit thereof, and did eat, and gave also unto her husband with her; and he did eat. And the eyes of them both were opened, and they knew that they were naked; and they sewed fig leaves together, and made themselves aprons. And they heard the voice of the Lord God walking in the garden in the cool of the day: and Adam and his wife hid themselves from the presence of the Lord God amongst the trees of the garden.

Genesis 3:6-8

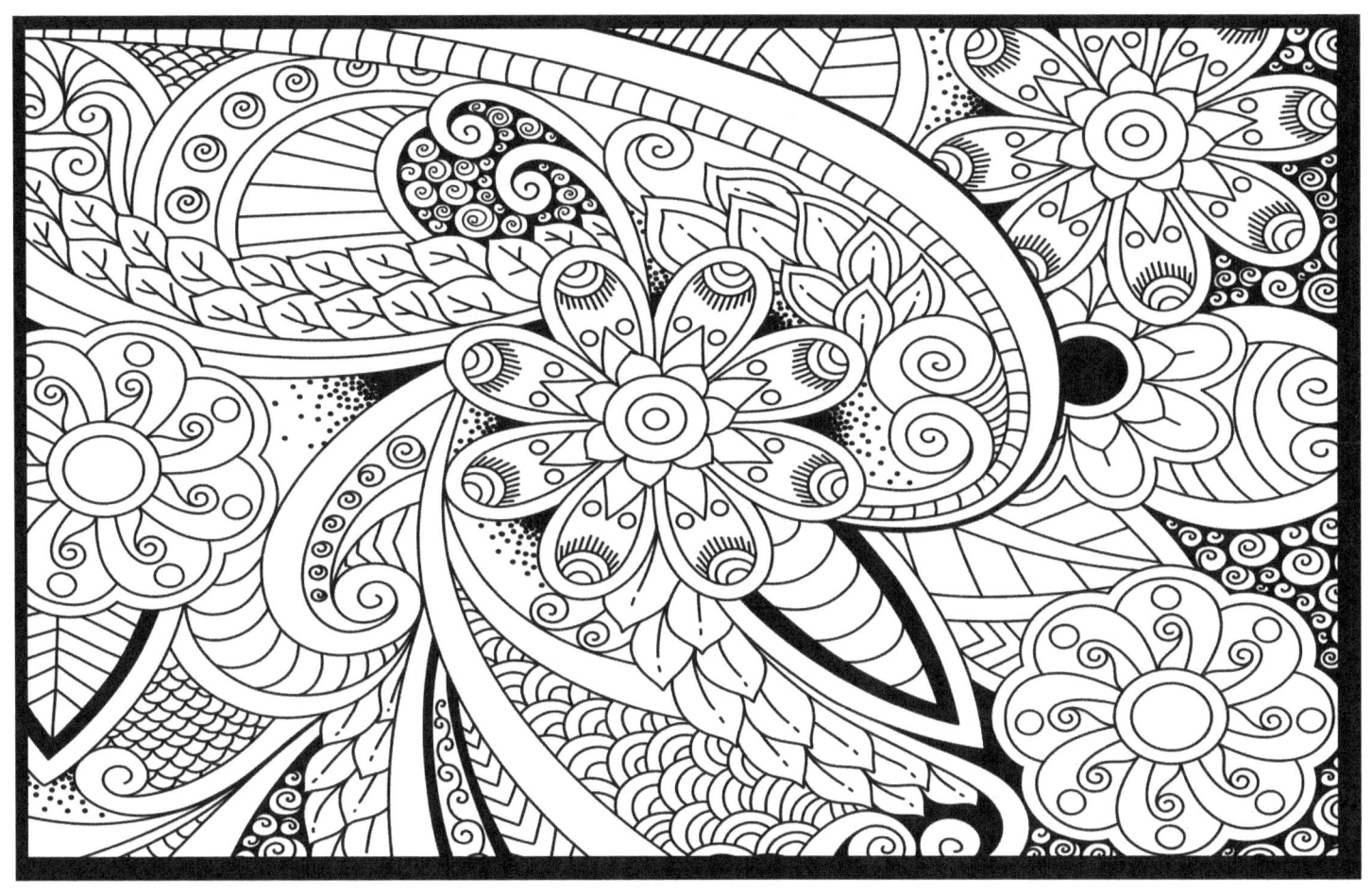

22. Fidelity is the best choice, not the only choice. Choose wisely.

Romans 12:1-2

Lord, help us to color our marriage with...

_____
_____
_____
_____
_____
_____
_____
_____
_____
_____
_____
_____

And I beseech you therefore, brethren, by the mercies of God, that ye present your bodies a living sacrifice, holy, acceptable unto God, which is your reasonable service. And be not conformed to this world: but be ye transformed by the renewing of your mind, that ye may prove what is that good, and acceptable, and perfect will of God.

Romans 12:1-2

Submit yourselves therefore to God.
Resist the devil, and he will flee from you.
Draw nigh to God, and he will draw nigh to you.
Cleanse your hands, ye sinners;
and purify your hearts, ye double-minded.

James 4:7-8

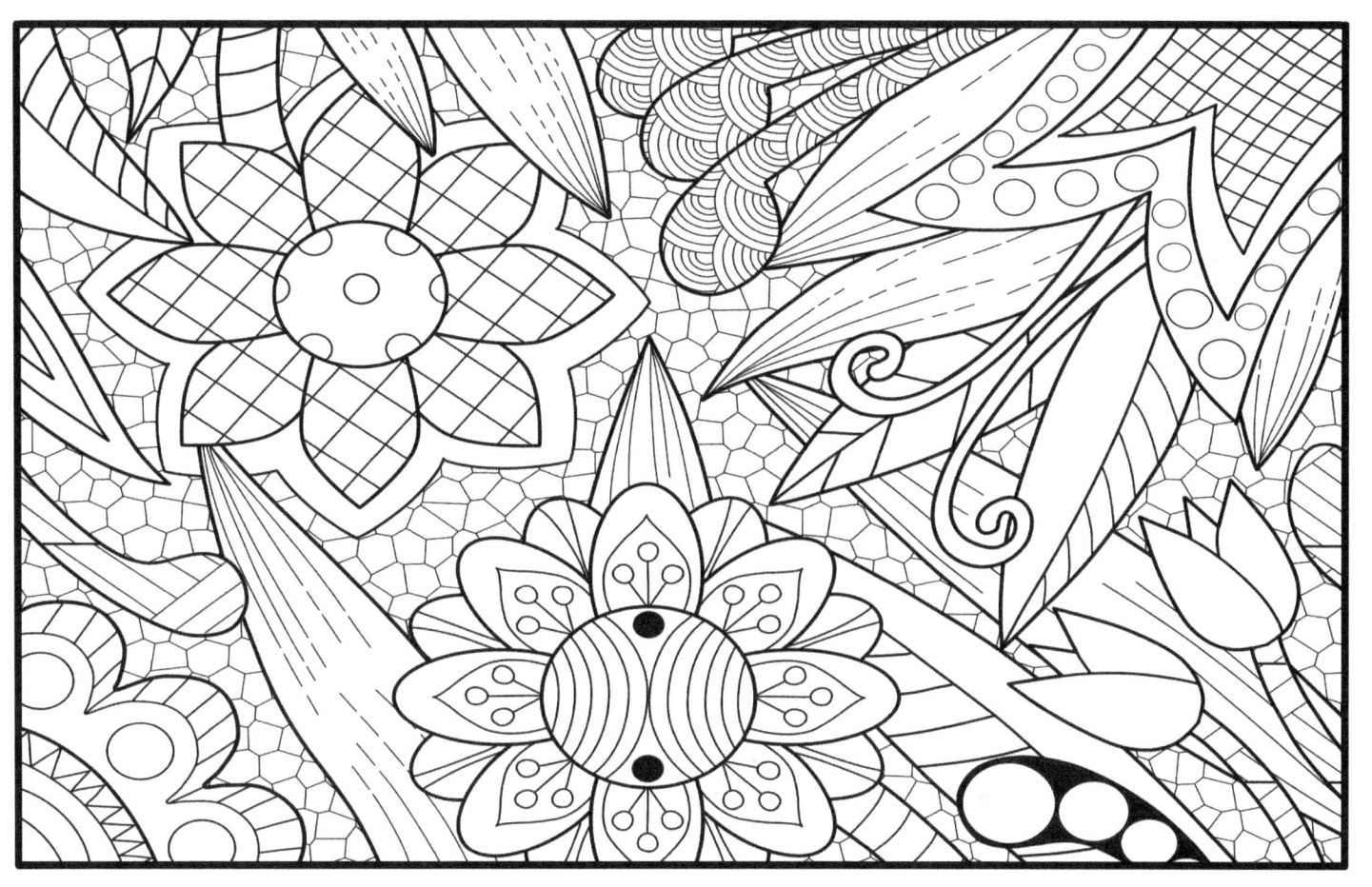

23. Make family decisions with wisdom and unity.
Psalm 133:1-3

Lord, help us to color our marriage with…

_____
_____
_____
_____
_____
_____
_____
_____
_____
_____
_____

Behold, how good and how pleasant it is

for brethren to dwell together in unity!

It is like the precious ointment upon the head,

that ran down upon the beard,

even Aaron's beard:

that went down to the skirts of his garments;

as the dew of Hermon,

and as the dew that descended upon the mountains of Zion:

for there the Lord commanded the blessing,

even life for evermore.

Psalm 133:1-3

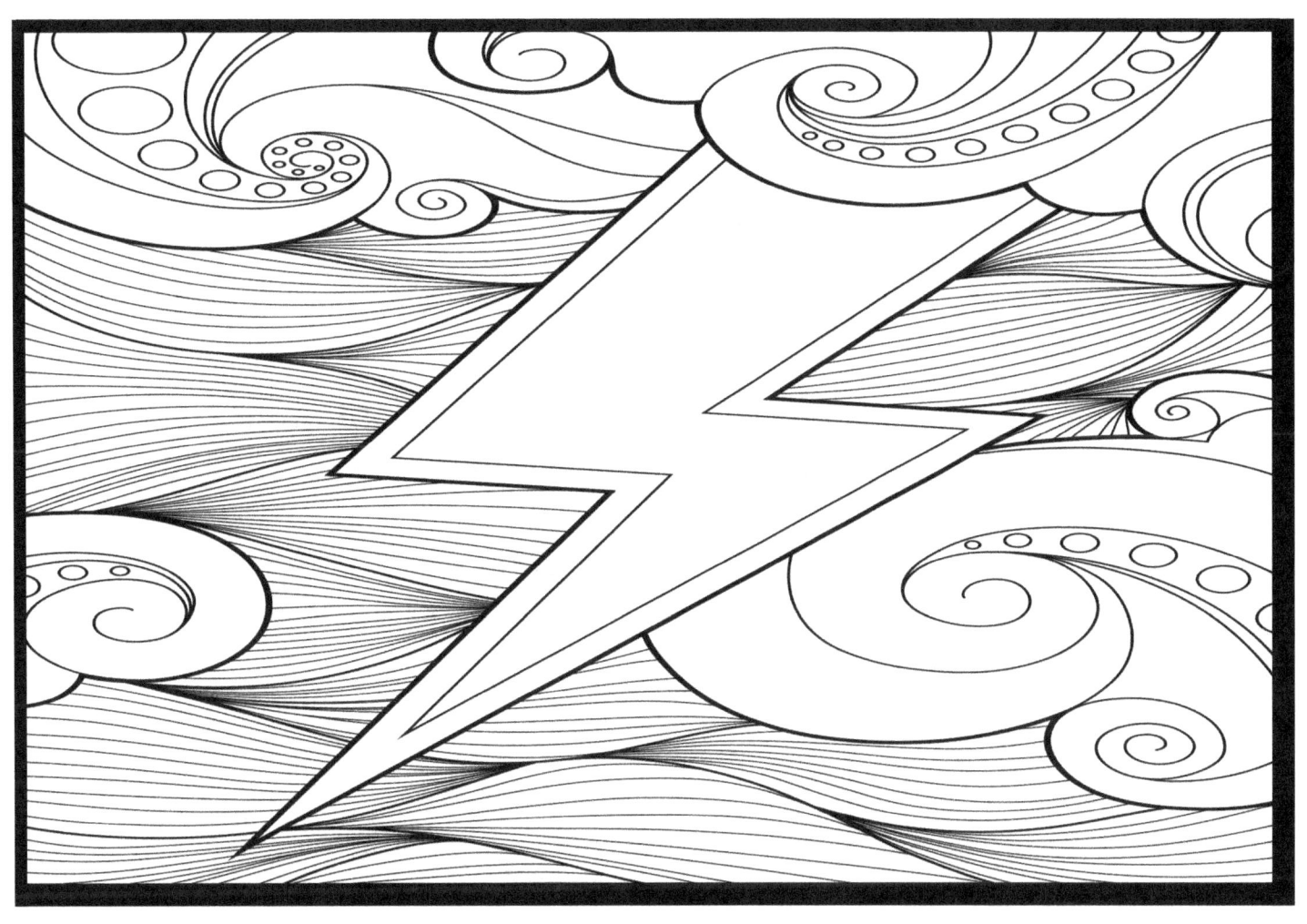

24. Know your "peacekeeping" plan in times of crisis.
Proverbs 15:1; Ecclesiastes 9:17-18

Lord, help us to color our marriage with...
_____
_____
_____
_____
_____
_____
_____
_____
_____
_____
_____
_____

A soft answer turneth away wrath:
but grievous words stir up anger.
Proverbs 15: 1

The words of wise men are heard in quiet more than the cry of
him that ruleth among fools. Wisdom is better than weapons
of war: but one sinner destroyeth much good.
Ecclesiastes 9:17-18

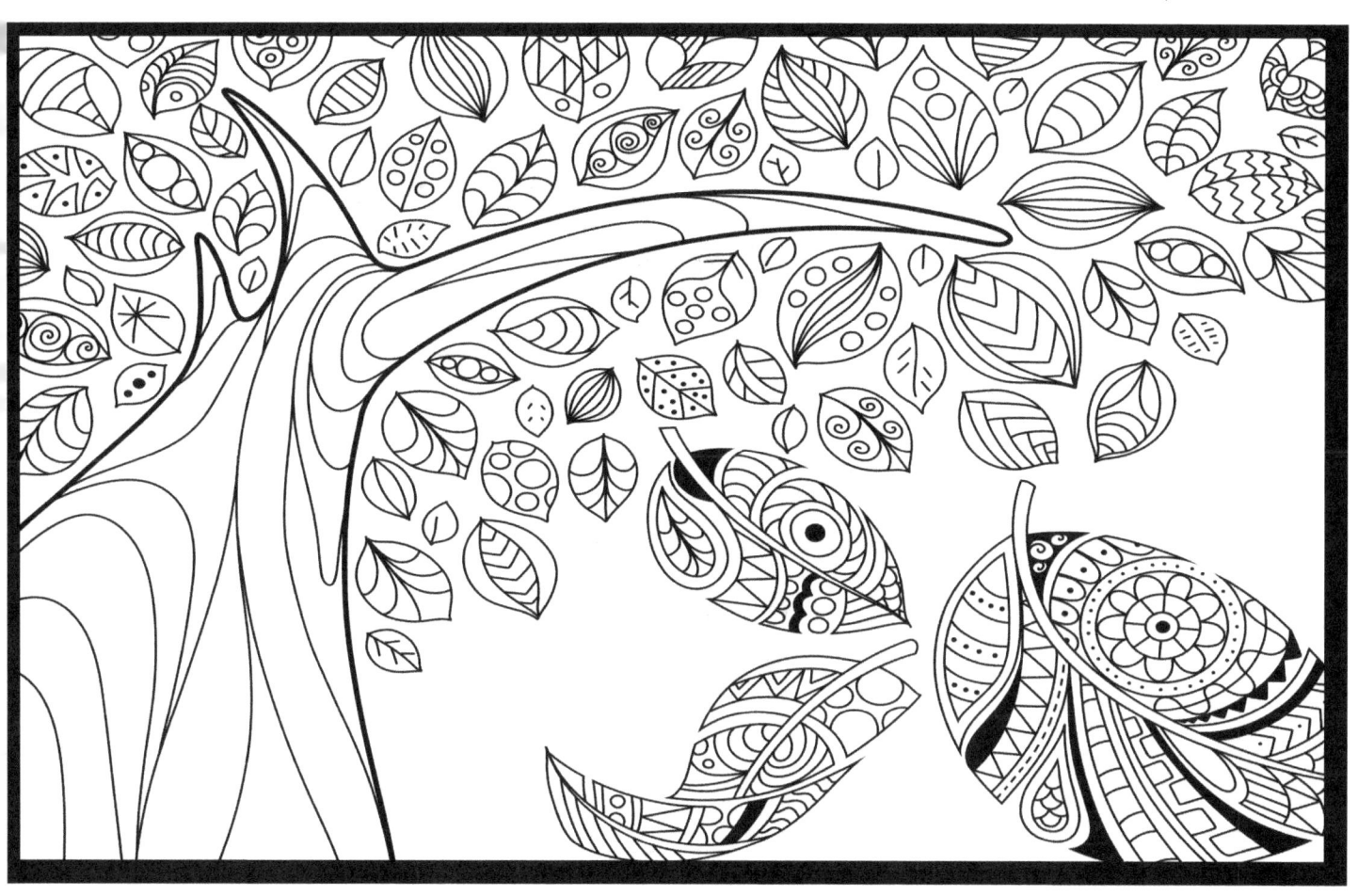

25. What you resist may be the thing you need the most.

Isaiah 43:18-19

Lord, help us to color our marriage with...

_____
_____
_____
_____
_____
_____
_____
_____
_____
_____
_____
_____

Remember ye not the former things,

neither consider the things of old.

Behold, I will do a new thing;

now it shall spring forth;

shall ye not know it?

I will even make a way

in the wilderness,

and rivers in the desert.

Isaiah 43:18-19

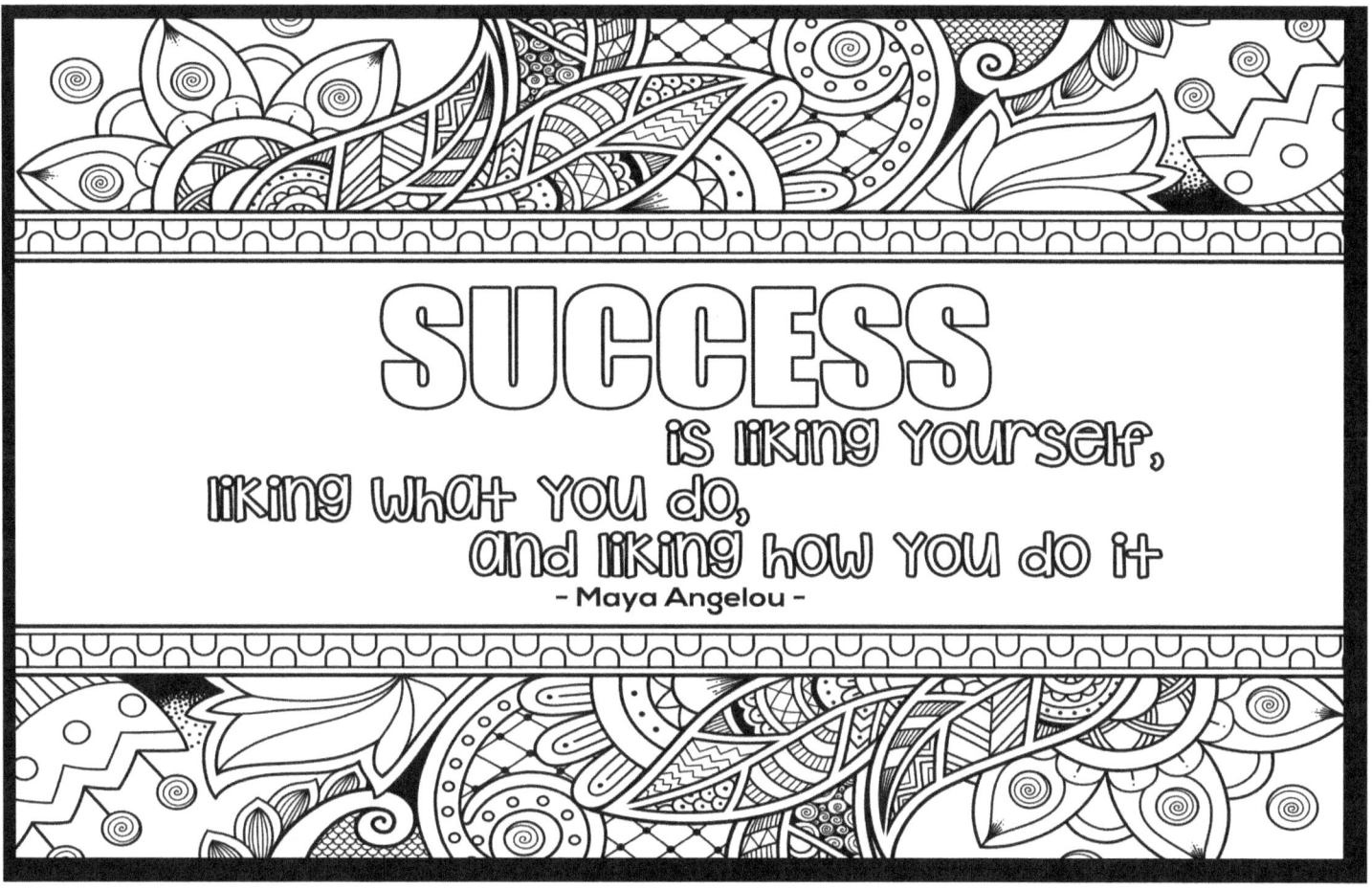

SUCCESS
is liking yourself,
liking what you do,
and liking how you do it
- Maya Angelou -

26. Don't get comfortable after a success.

Philippians 3:12-14

Lord, help us to color our marriage with...

_____
_____
_____
_____
_____
_____
_____
_____
_____
_____
_____

Not as though I had already attained, either were already perfect: but I follow after, if that I may apprehend that for which also I am apprehended of Christ Jesus. ₁Brethren, I count not myself to have apprehended: but this one thing I do, forgetting those things which are behind, and reaching forth unto those things which are before. I press toward the mark for the prize of the high calling of God in Christ Jesus.

Philippians 3:12-14

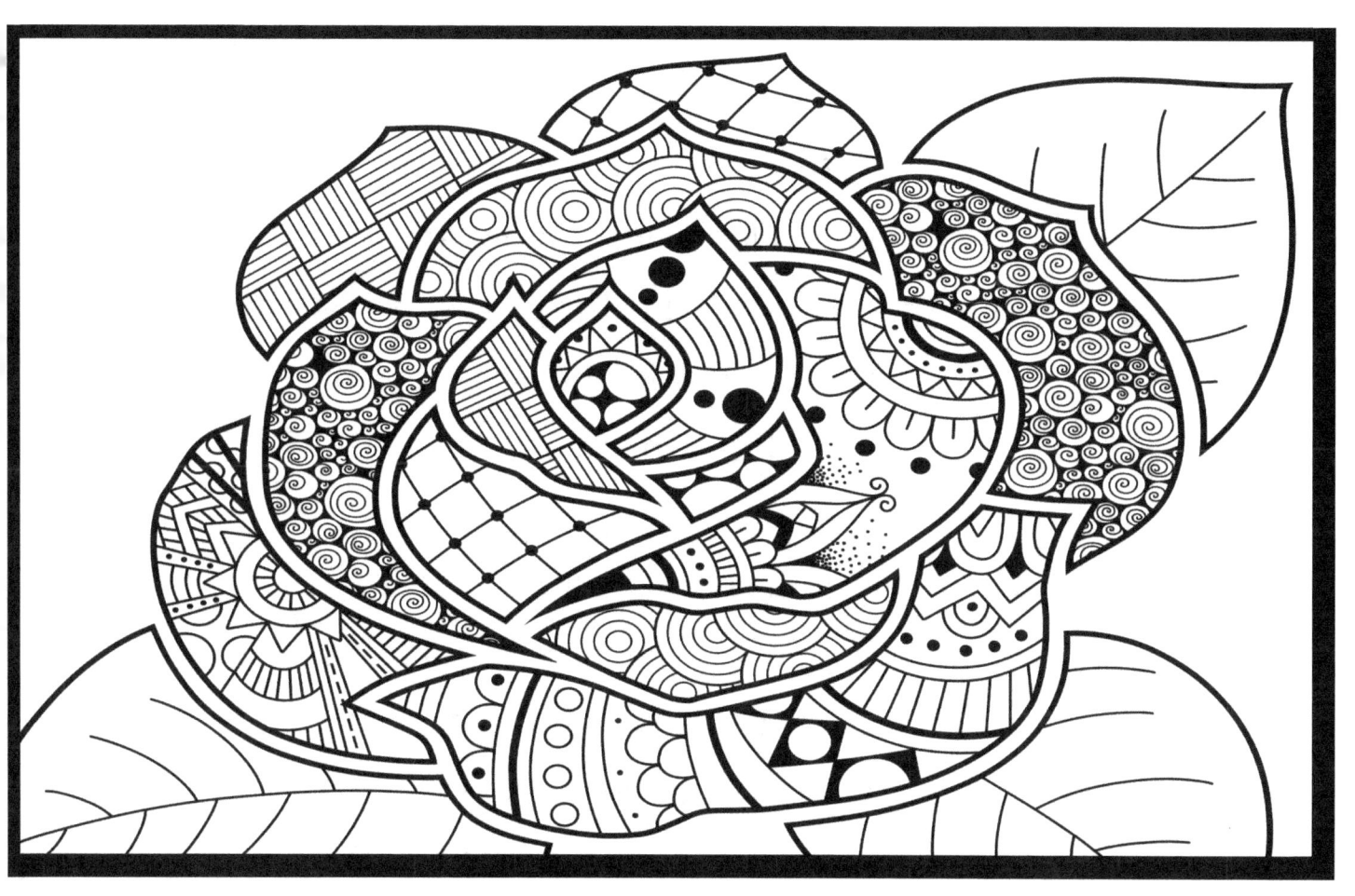

27. All communication is not effective.
Proverbs 12:17-18; 15:2-4

Lord, help us to color our marriage with...
_____
_____
_____
_____
_____
_____
_____
_____
_____
_____

He that speaketh truth showeth forth righteousness:

but a false witness deceit.

There is that speaketh like the piercings of a sword:

but the tongue of the wise is health.

Proverbs 12:17-18

The tongue of the wise useth knowledge aright:

but the mouth of fools poureth out foolishness.

The eyes of the Lord are in every place,

beholding the evil and the good.

A wholesome tongue is a tree of life:

but perverseness therein is a breach in the spirit.

Proverbs 15:2-4

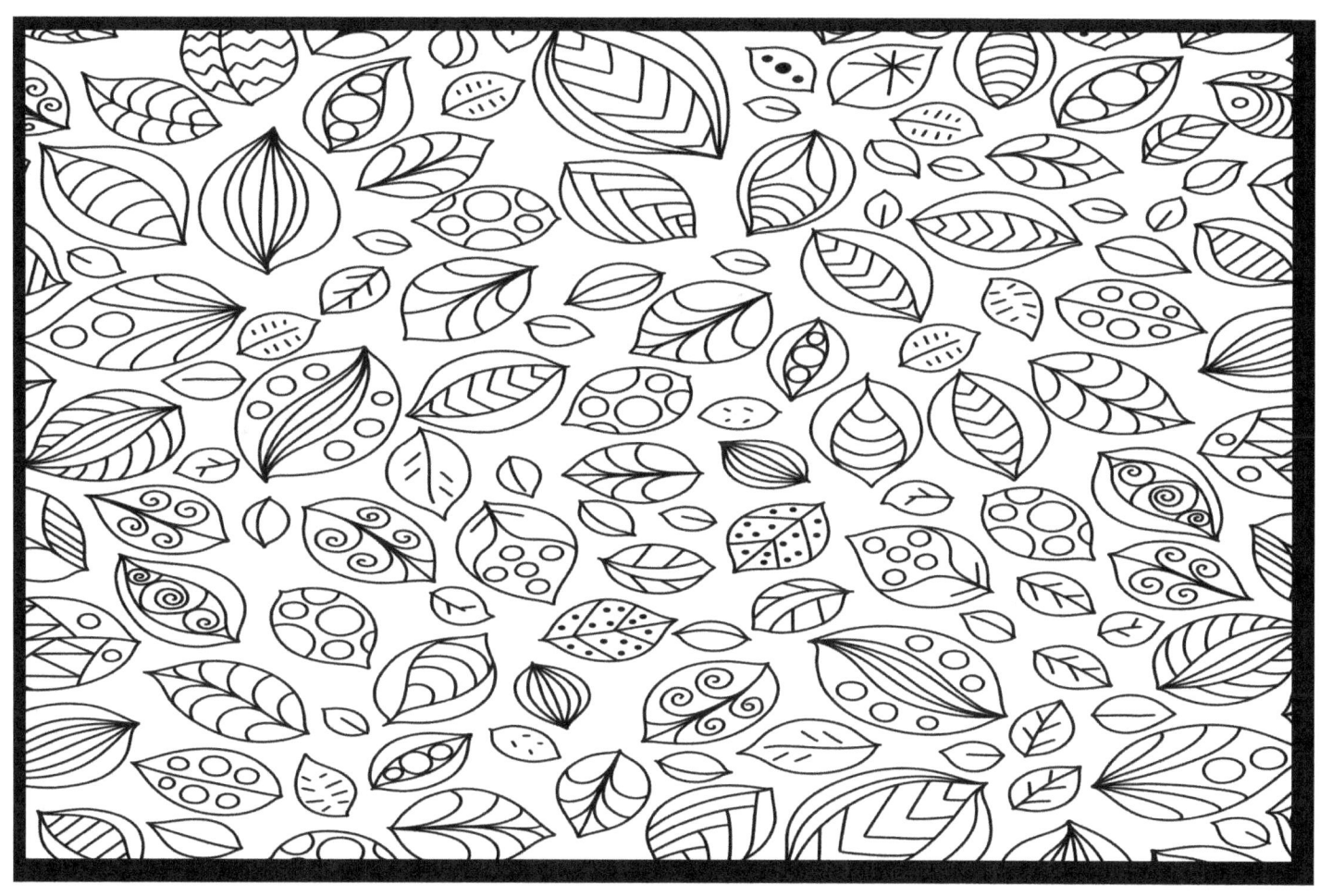

28. Other people may need more of your spouse's attention than you.

Galatians 6:9-10

Lord, help us to color our marriage with...

_____
_____
_____
_____
_____
_____
_____
_____
_____
_____
_____
_____

And let us not be weary in well doing: for in due season we shall reap, if we faint not. As we have therefore opportunity, let us do good unto all men, especially unto them who are of the household of faith.

Galatians 6:9-10

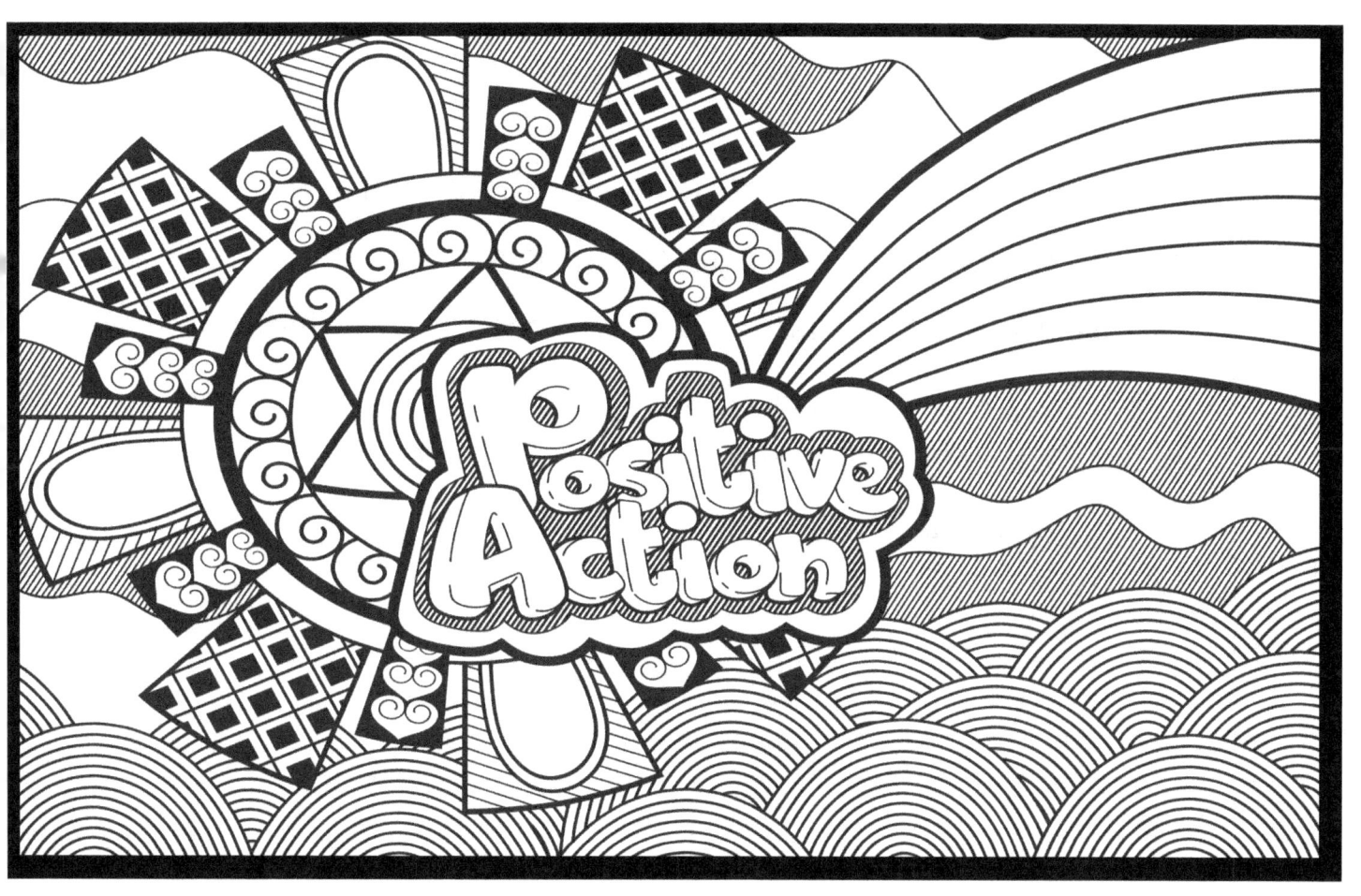

29. Learn to give and receive sincere tough love.

I Corinthians 13:4-7

Lord, help us to color our marriage with...

_____
_____
_____
_____
_____
_____
_____
_____
_____
_____
_____
_____

Charity suffereth long, and is kind; charity envieth not; charity
vaunteth not itself, is not puffed up, doth not behave itself
unseemly, seeketh not her own, is not easily provoked,
thinketh no evil; rejoiceth not in iniquity,
but rejoiceth in the truth; beareth all things,
believeth all things, hopeth all things,
endureth all things.
I Corinthians 13:4-7

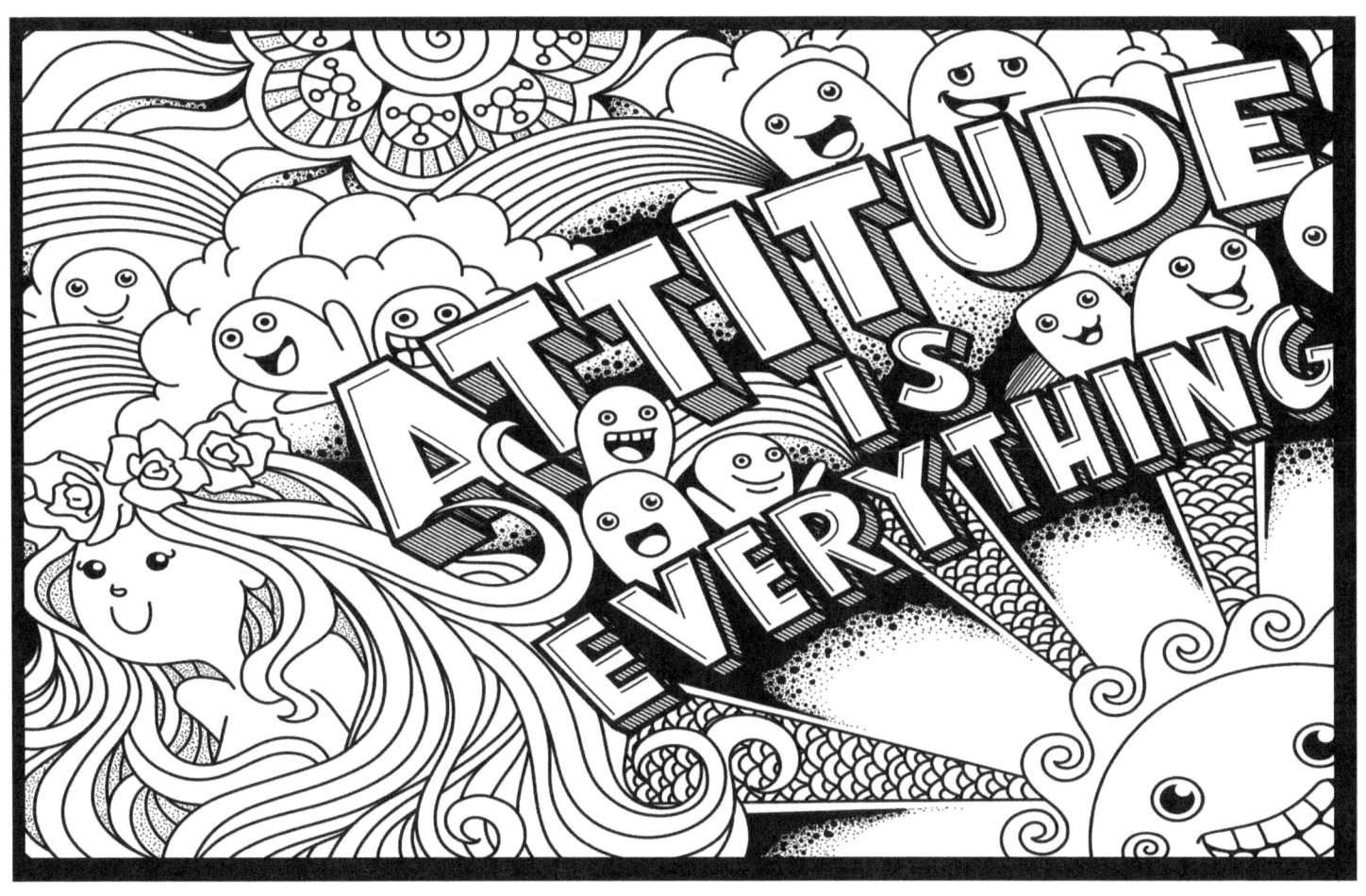

30. It's not the size of the "BUTS" that matter, it's how you handle them.

James 1:2-5

Lord, help us to color our marriage with...

_____
_____
_____
_____
_____
_____
_____
_____
_____
_____
_____
_____

My brethren, count it all joy when ye fall into divers temptations; knowing this, that the trying of your faith worketh patience. But let patience have her perfect work, that ye may be perfect and entire, wanting nothing. If any of you lack wisdom, let him ask of God, that giveth to all men liberally, and upbraideth not; and it shall be given him.

James 1:2-5

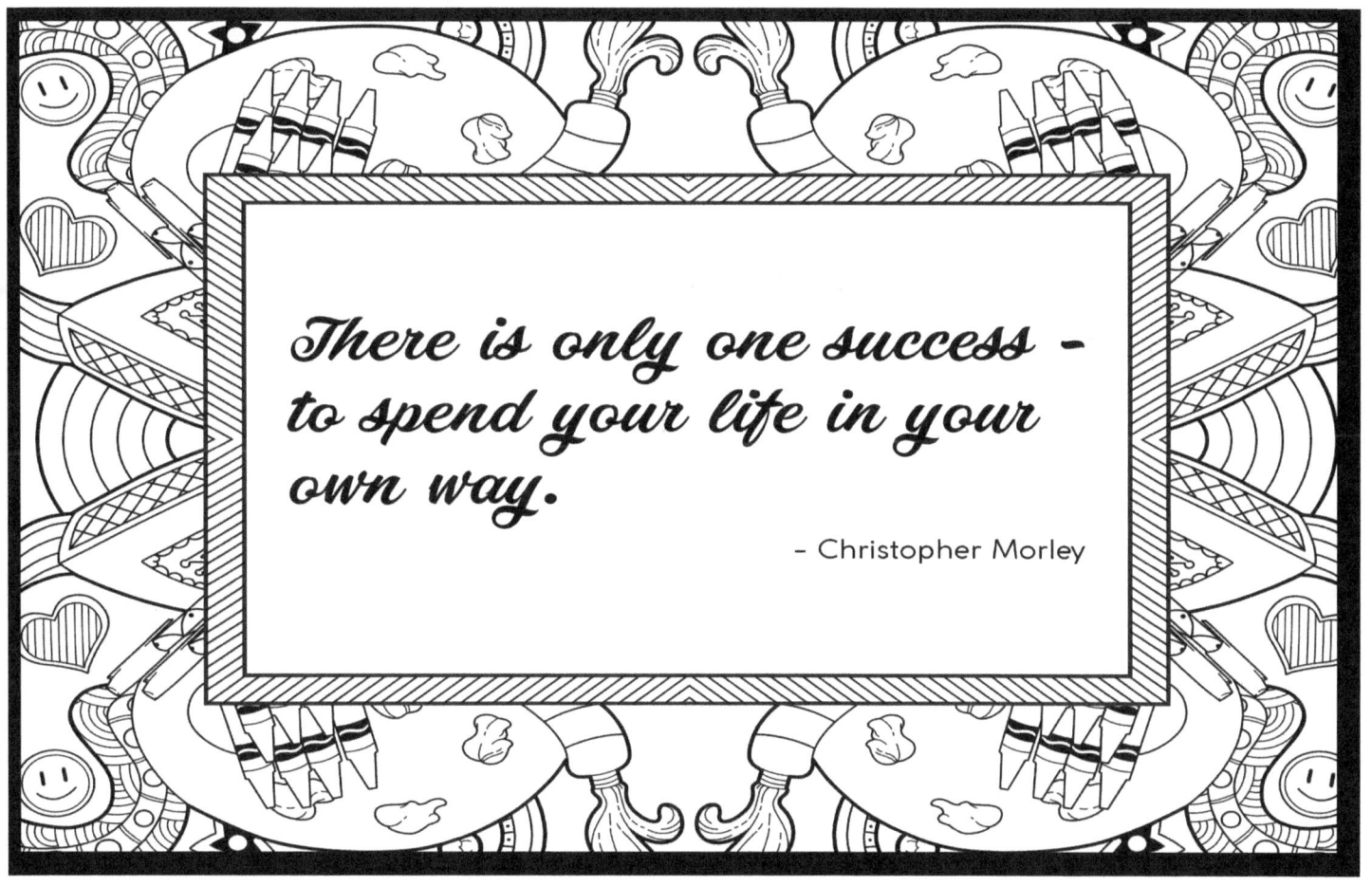

There is only one success - to spend your life in your own way.

– Christopher Morley

31. Don't let others force their dreams and desires on your relationship goals.

Psalm 37:4-5

Lord, help us to color our marriage with…

Delight thyself also in the Lord;

and he shall give thee the desires of thine heart.

Commit thy way unto the Lord;

trust also in him; and he shall bring it to pass.

Psalm 37:4-5

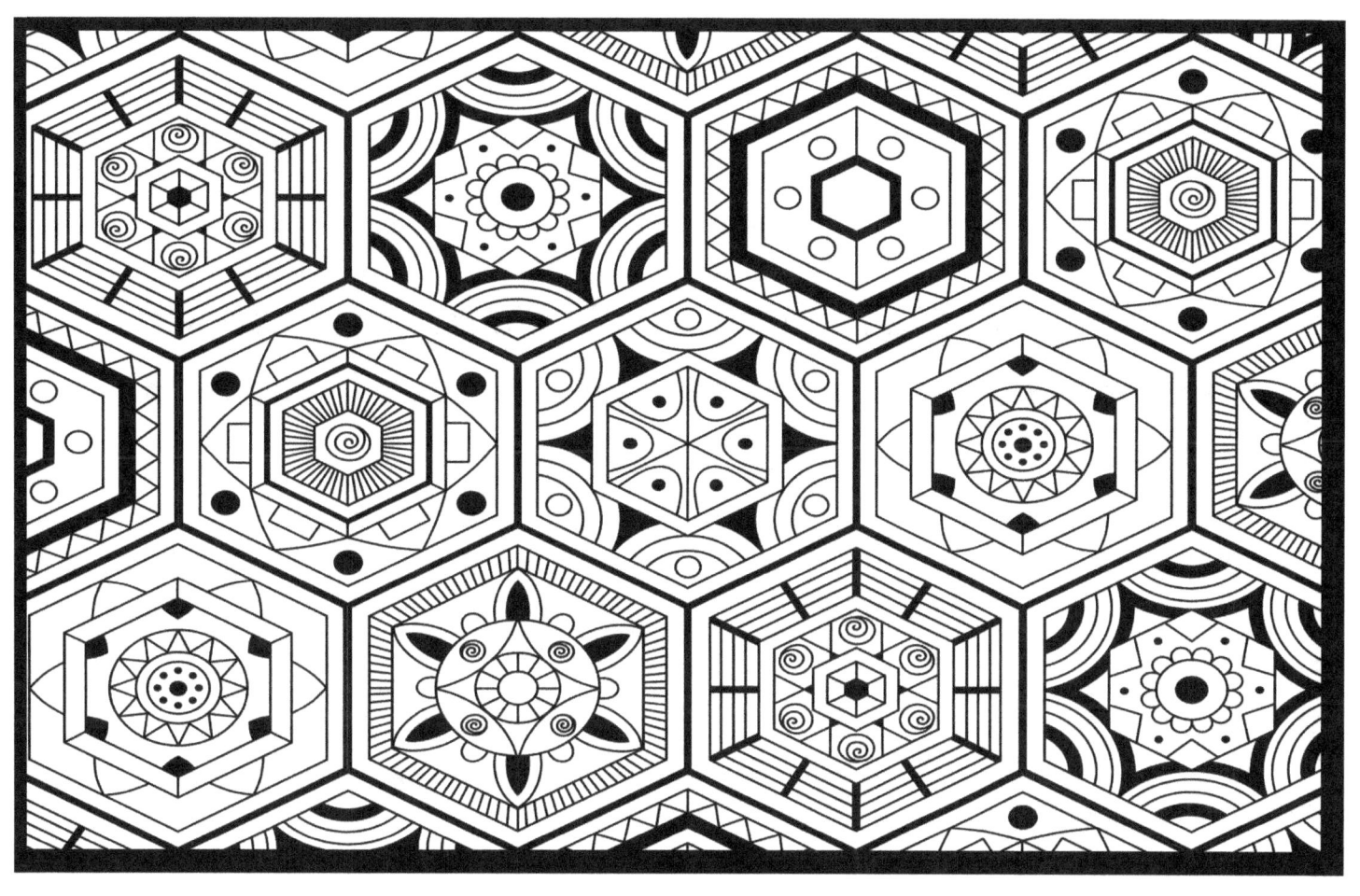

32. Technology is not a replacement for reality.
I Corinthians 6:12

Lord, help us to color our marriage with...

All things are lawful unto me, but all things are not expedient:
all things are lawful for me, but I will not be brought under the
power of any.
I Corinthians 6:12

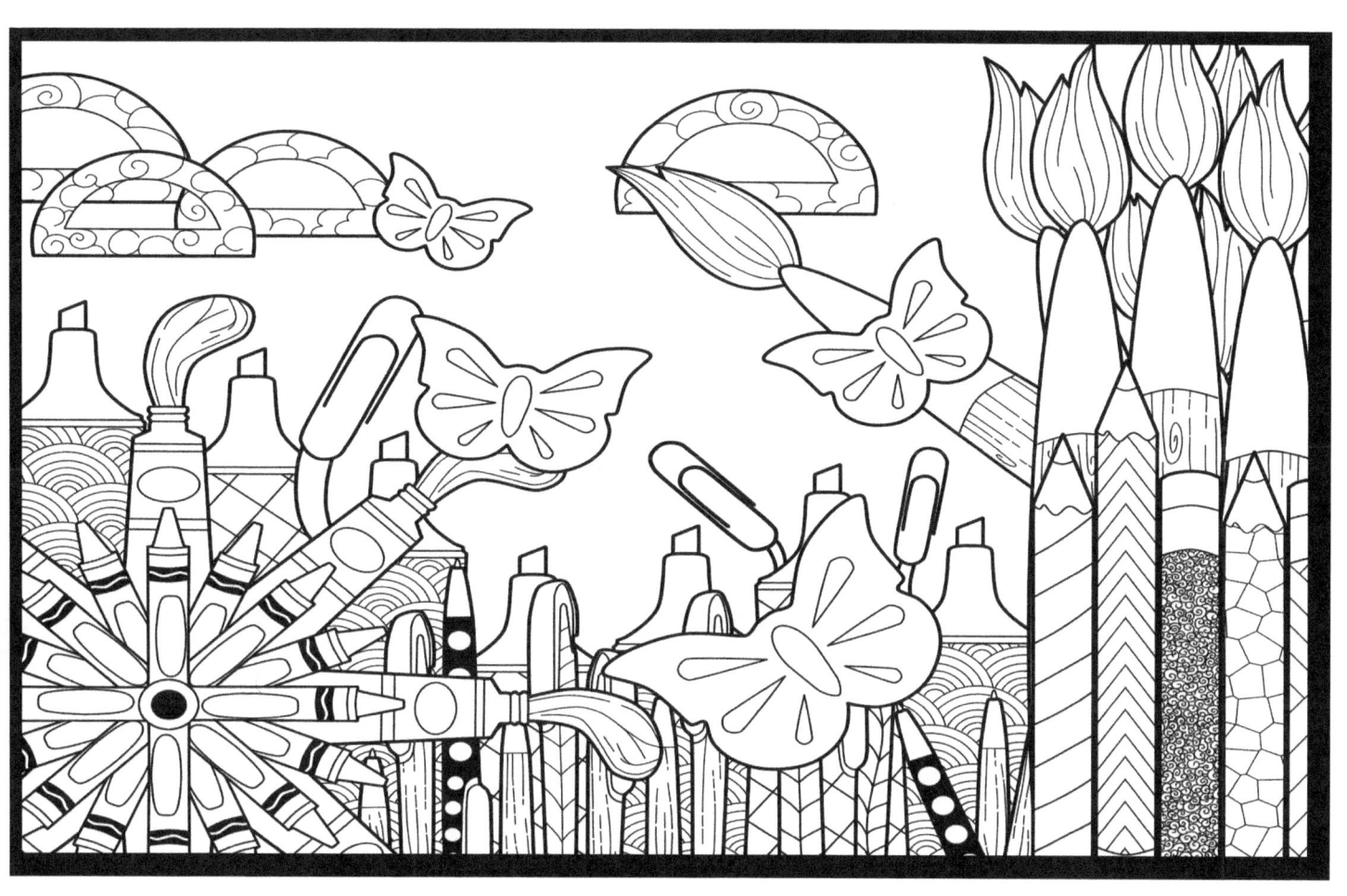

33. Adjust to accommodate your spouse's changing needs.
Ephesians 4:2-5

Lord, help us to color our marriage with…

_____
_____
_____
_____
_____
_____
_____
_____
_____
_____
_____
_____

...with all lowliness and meekness, with long-suffering, for-bearing one another in love; endeavoring to keep the unity of the Spirit in the bond of peace. There is one body, and one Spir-it, even as ye are called in one hope of your calling; one Lord, one faith, one baptism...

Ephesians 4:2-5

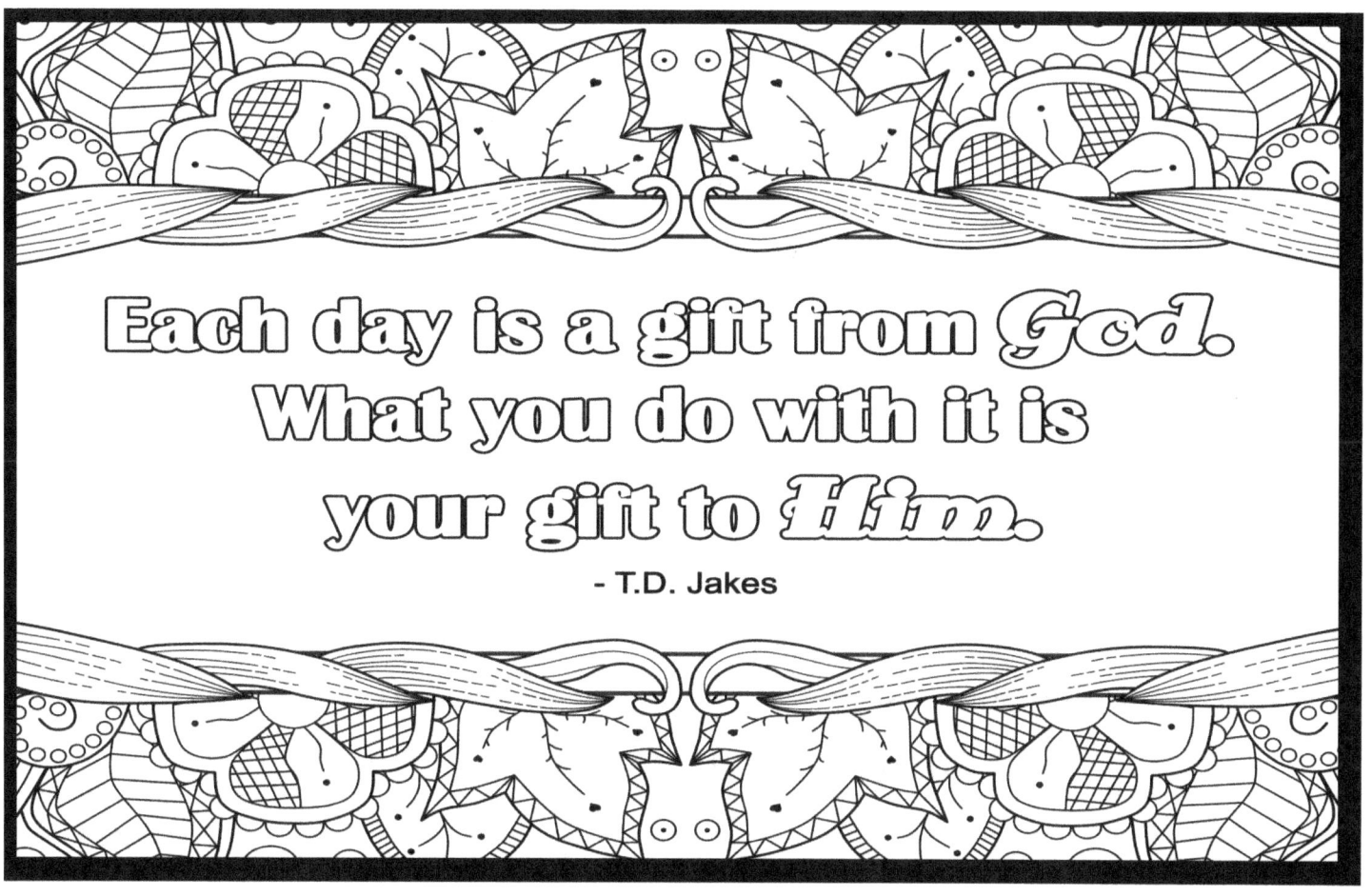

Each day is a gift from *God.*
What you do with it is
your gift to *Him.*

- T.D. Jakes

34. Don't go too fast and miss the signs.

Ecclesiastes 3:1; Luke 10:40-42

Lord, help us to color our marriage with...

_____
_____
_____
_____
_____
_____
_____
_____
_____
_____
_____
_____

To every thing there is a season, and a time to every purpose under the heaven...

Ecclesiastes 3:1

But Martha was cumbered about much serving, and came to him, and said, Lord, dost thou not care that my sister hath left me to serve alone? bid her therefore that she help me. And Jesus answered and said unto her, Martha, Martha, thou art careful and troubled about many things: but one thing is needful; and Mary hath chosen that good part, which shall not be taken away from her.

Luke 10:40-42

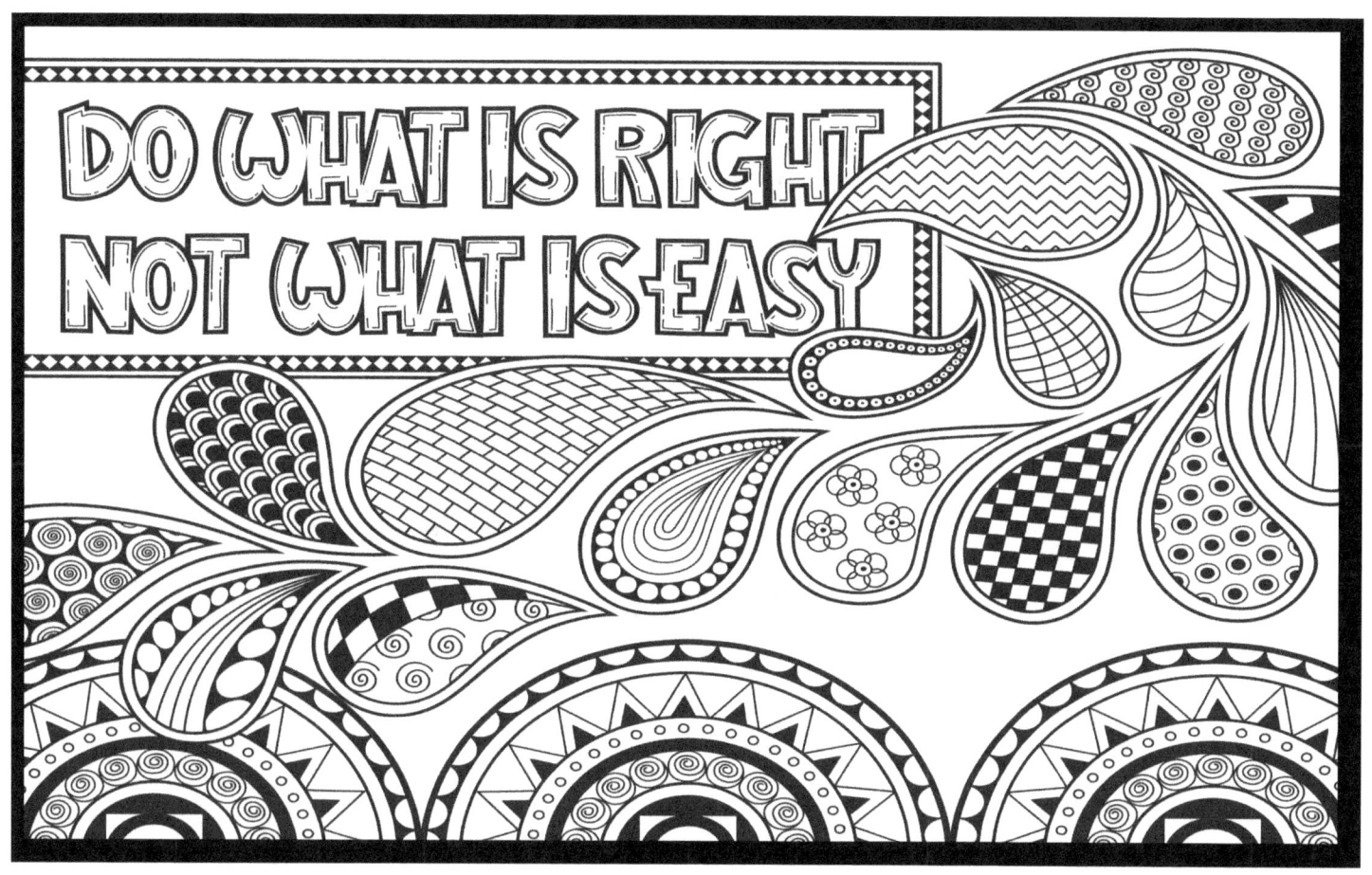

35. Men have the power of authority, women have the power of influence. Use your power wisely.

I Corinthians 11:3; Proverbs 14:1

Lord, help us to color our marriage with...

_____
_____
_____
_____
_____
_____
_____
_____
_____
_____
_____

But I would have you know, that the head of every man is
Christ; and the head of the woman is the man;
and the head of Christ is God.
I Corinthians 11:3

Every wise woman buildeth her house:
but the foolish plucketh it down with her hands.
Proverbs 14:1

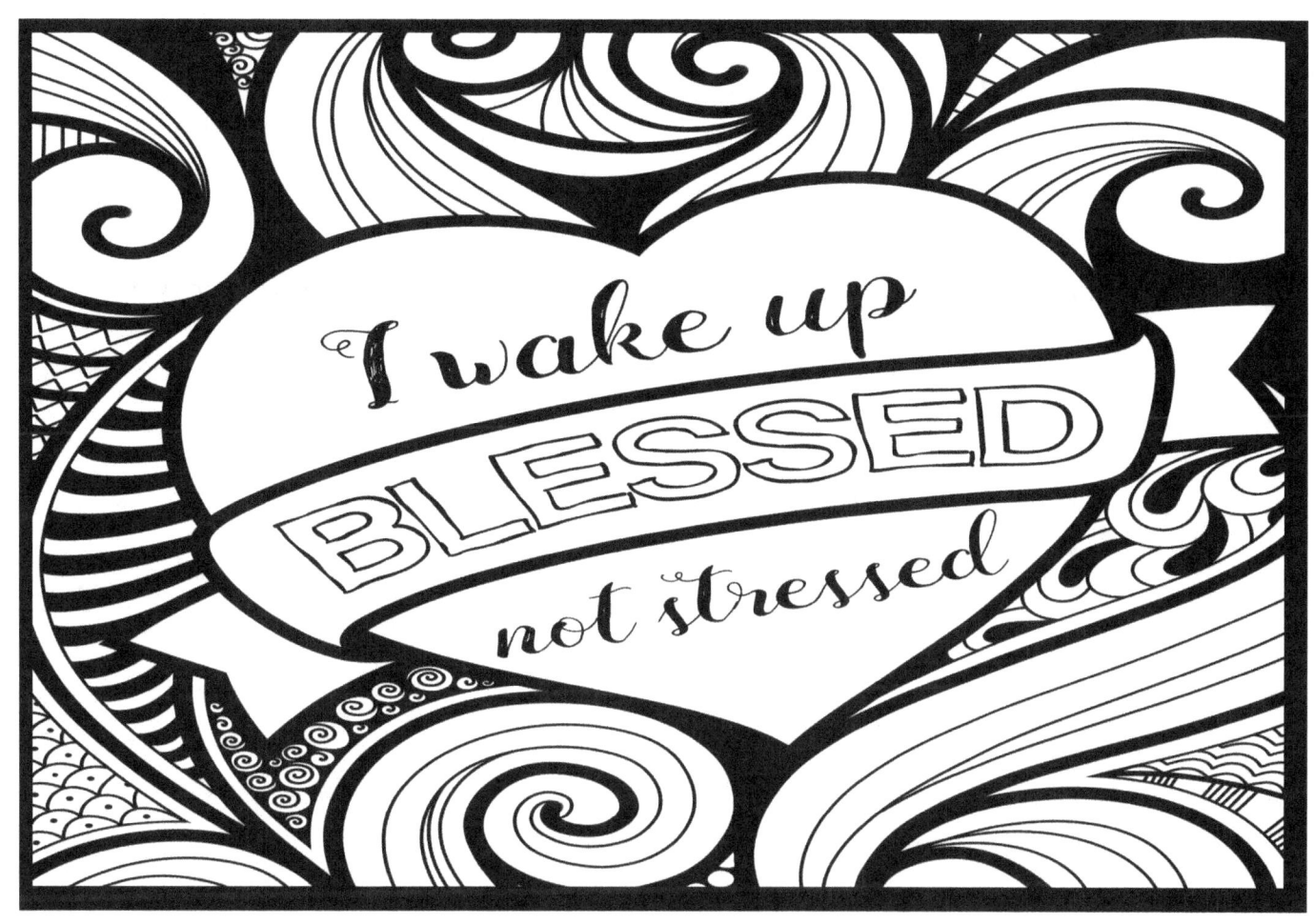

36. Plans may fail. It's your response that makes the difference.
I Thessalonians 5:16-18

Lord, help us to color our marriage with...

Rejoice evermore. Pray without ceasing. In every thing give
thanks: for this is the will of God in
Christ Jesus concerning you.
I Thessalonians 5:16-18

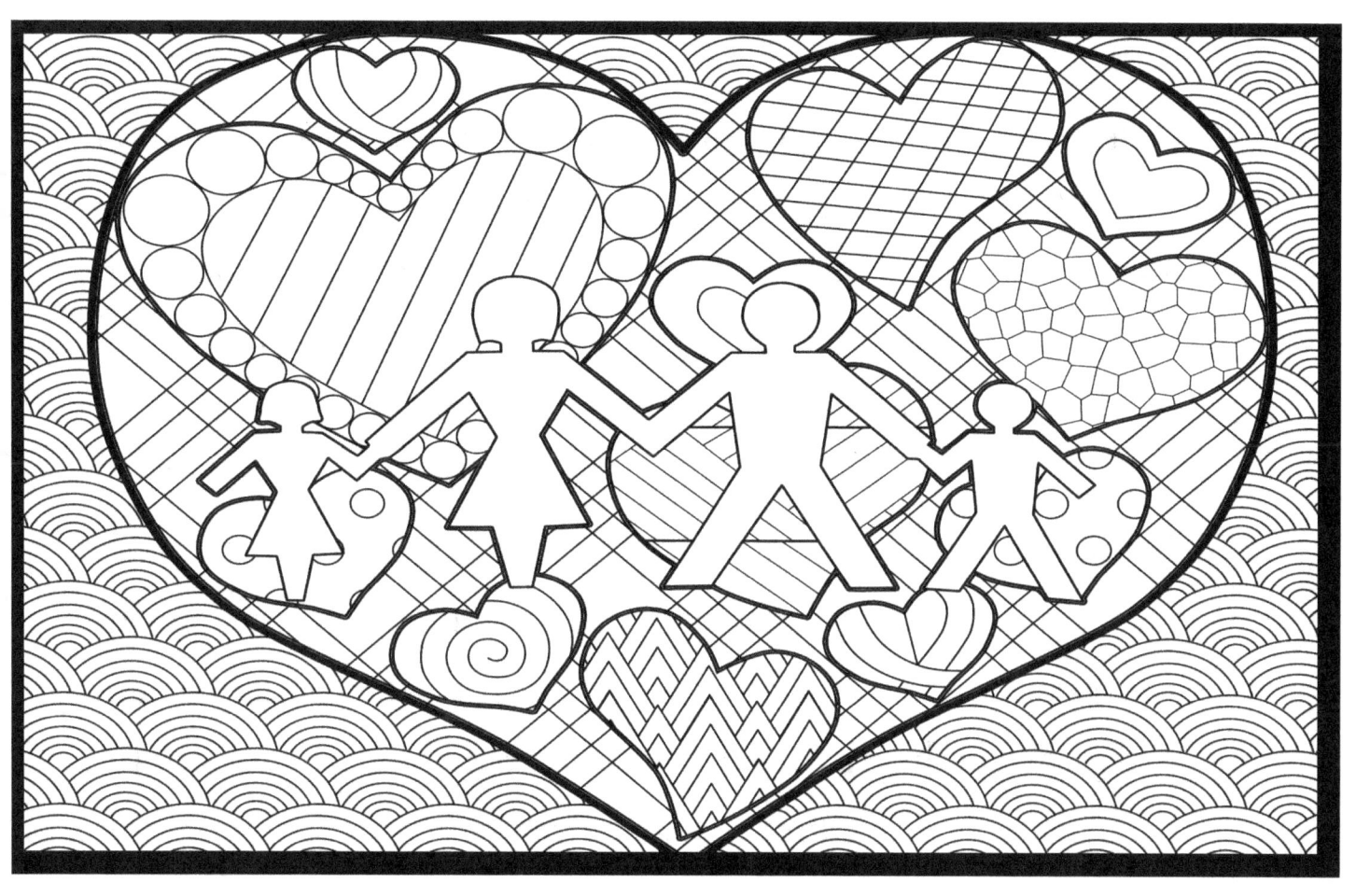

37. Protect the most vulnerable things in times of crisis.

Nehemiah 4:1-23

Lord, help us to color our marriage with...

... Be not ye afraid of them: remember the Lord, which is great and terrible, and fight for your brethren, your sons, and your daughters, your wives, and your houses. ... And it came to pass from that time forth, that the half of my servants wrought in the work, and the other half of them held both the spears, the shields, and the bows, and the habergeons; and the rulers were behind all the house of Judah. They which builded on the wall, and they that bare burdens, with those that laded, every one with one of his hands wrought in the work, and with the other hand held a weapon. For the builders, every one had his sword girded by his side, and so builded. And he that sounded the trumpet was by me.

Nehemiah 4:1-23

(Please read the passage in its entirety)

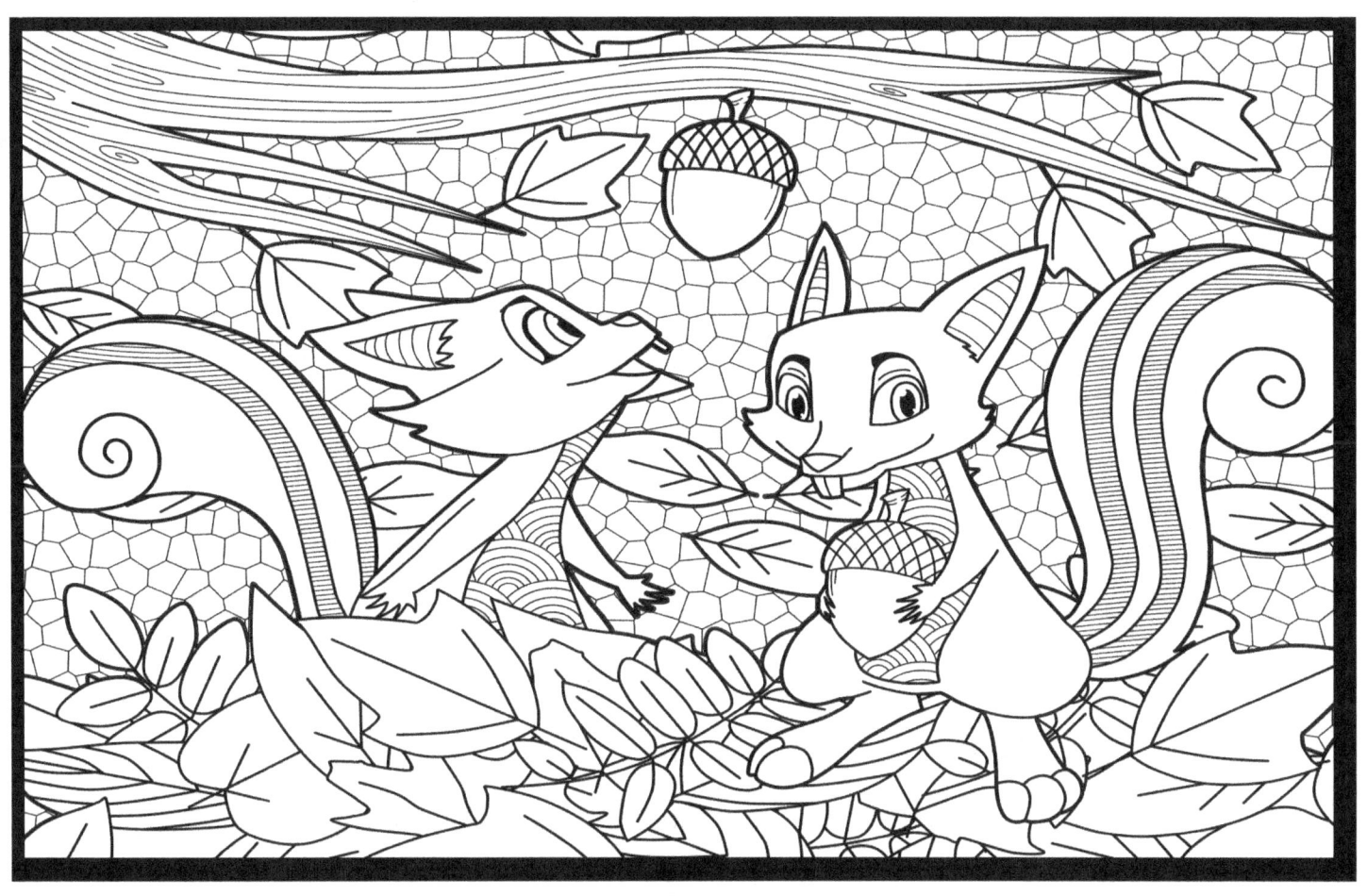

38. Lack of priorities is a breeding ground for chaos and confusion.
Luke 10:38-42

Lord, help us to color our marriage with...

Now it came to pass, as they went, that he entered into a certain village: and a certain woman named Martha received him into her house. And she had a sister called Mary, which also sat at Jesus' feet, and heard his word. But Martha was cumbered about much serving, and came to him, and said, Lord, dost thou not care that my sister hath left me to serve alone? Bid her therefore that she help me. And Jesus answered and said unto her, Martha, Martha, thou art careful and troubled about many things: but one thing is needful; and Mary hath chosen that good part, which shall not be taken away from her.

Luke 10:38-42

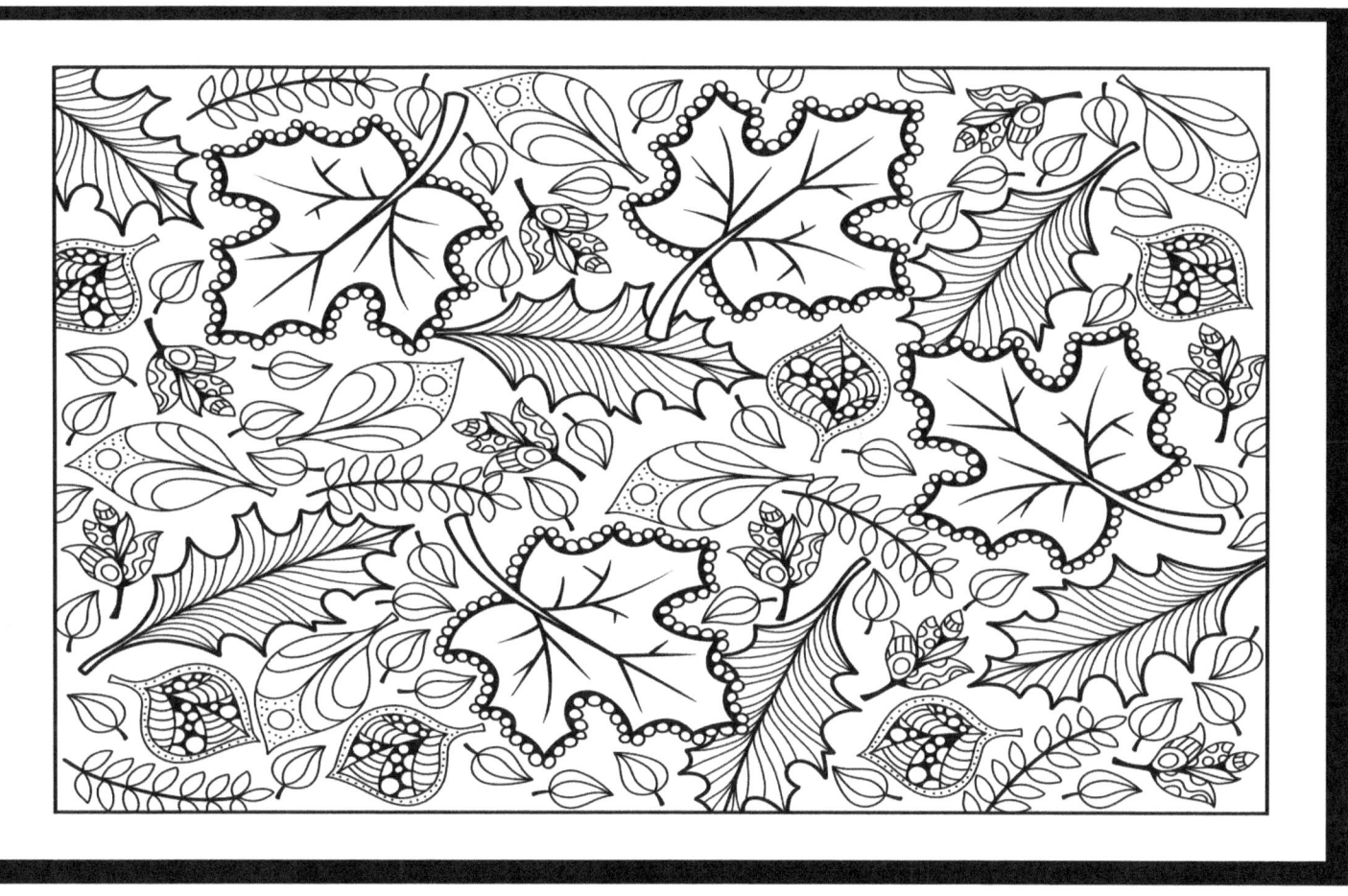

39. Consistent communication is key to avoiding a crisis.

James 1:19

Lord, help us to color our marriage with...

_____

_____

_____

_____

_____

_____

_____

_____

_____

_____

_____

Wherefore, my beloved brethren, let every man be swift to
hear, slow to speak, slow to wrath...

James 1:19

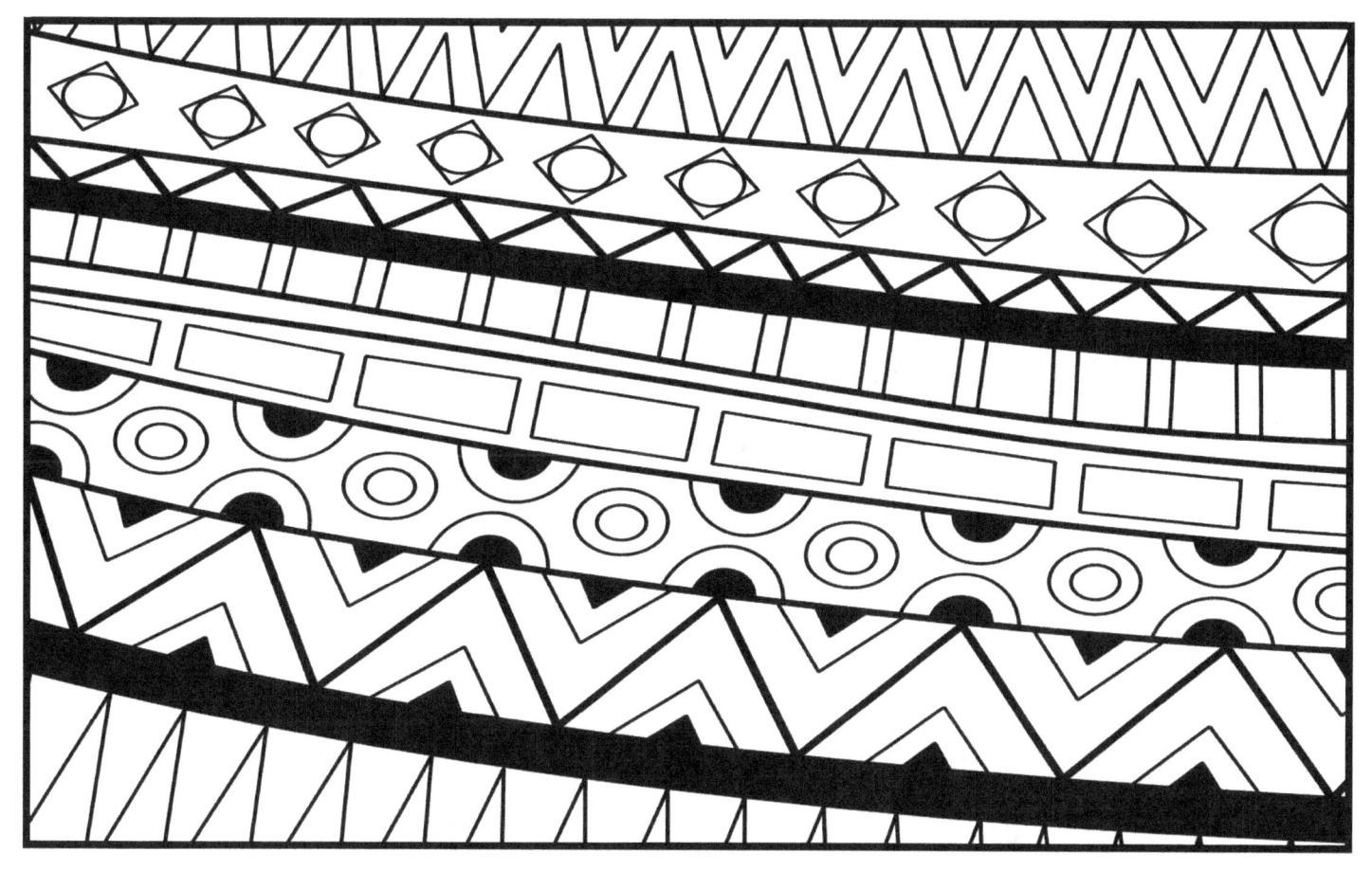

40. Major change is sometimes necessary for growth.

Genesis 12:1-3; Matthew 4:18-20

Lord, help us to color our marriage with...

_____

_____

_____

_____

_____

_____

_____

_____

_____

_____

_____

Now the Lord had said unto Abram, Get thee out of thy country, and from thy kindred, and from thy father's house, unto a land that I will show thee: and I will make of thee a great nation, and I will bless thee, and make thy name great; and thou shalt be a blessing: and I will bless them that bless thee, and curse him that curseth thee: and in thee shall all families of the earth be blessed.

Genesis 12:1-3

And Jesus, walking by the sea of Galilee, saw two brethren, Simon called Peter, and Andrew his brother, casting a net into the sea: for they were fishers. And he saith unto them, Follow me, and I will make you fishers of men. And they straightway left their nets, and followed him.

Matthew 4:18-20

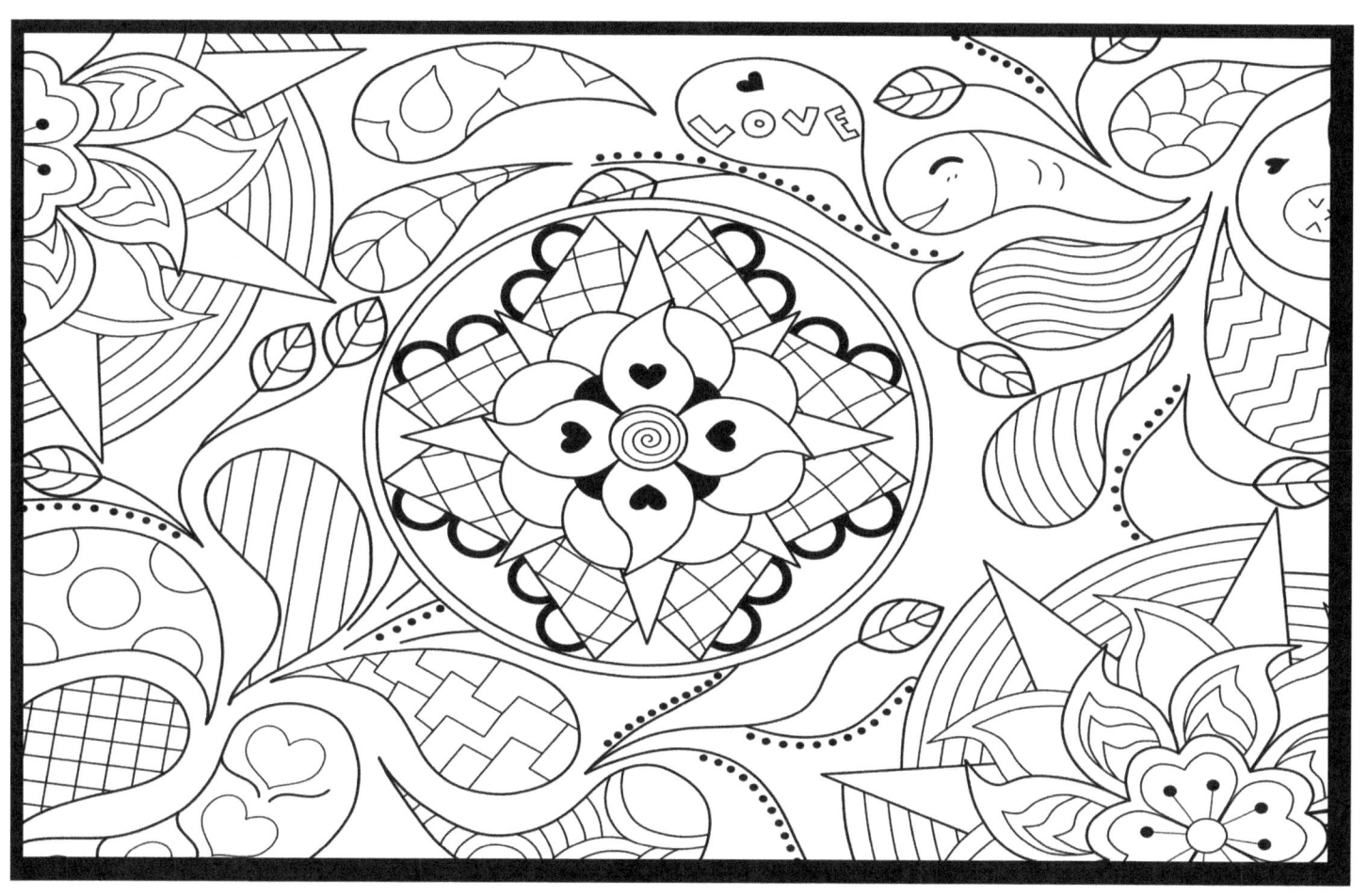

41. Choose marriage models wisely.
I Corinthians 11:1

Lord, help us to color our marriage with...

_____
_____
_____
_____
_____
_____
_____
_____
_____
_____
_____

Be ye followers of me, even as I also am of Christ.

I Corinthians 11:1

_____

_____

_____

_____

_____

_____

_____

_____

_____

_____

_____

_____

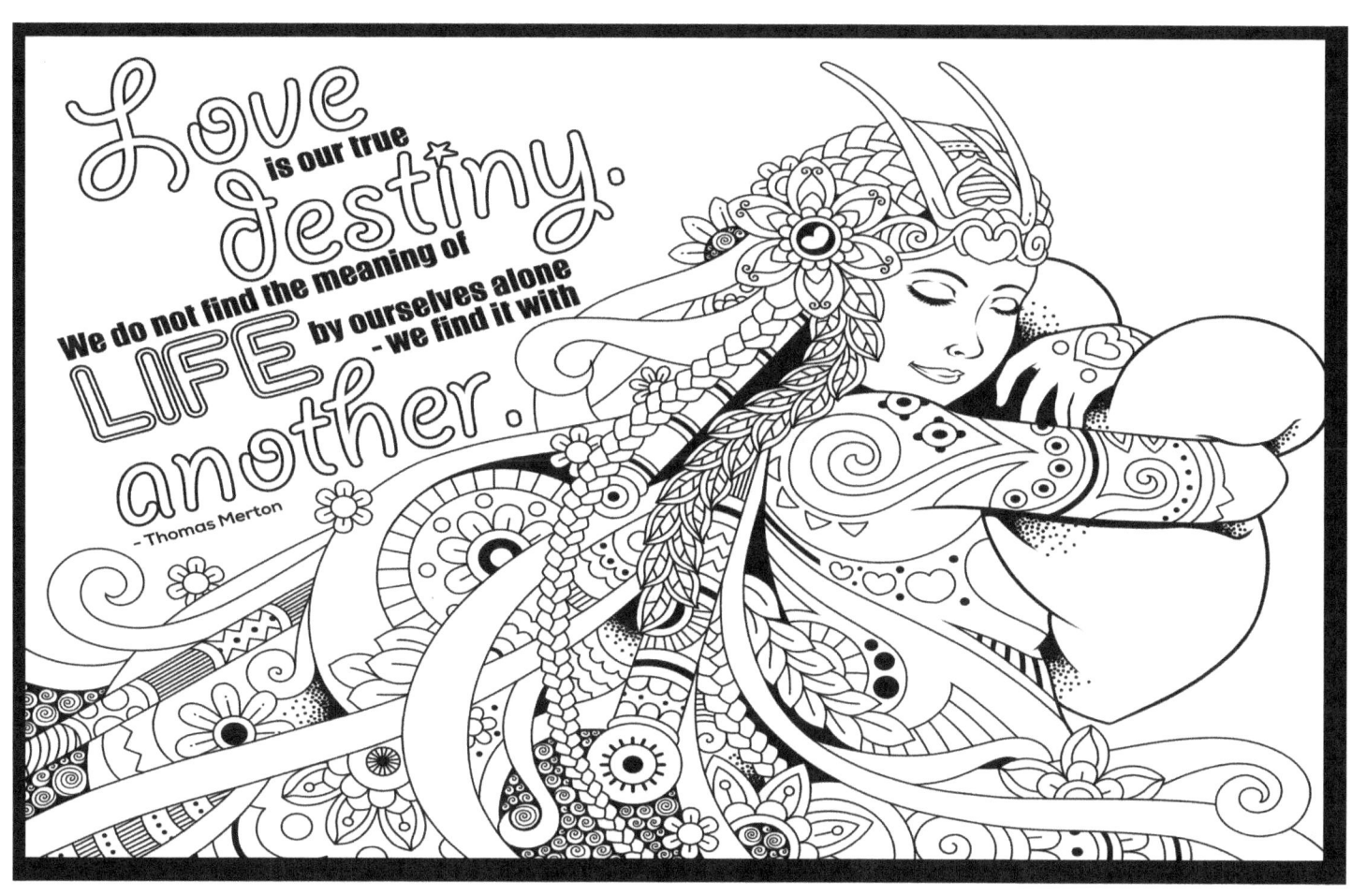

Love is our true destiny.
We do not find the meaning of LIFE by ourselves alone - we find it with another.
- Thomas Merton

42. Don't let anger, and pride keep your heart cold toward your spouse.

Ephesians 4:26-27

Lord, help us to color our marriage with...

Be ye angry, and sin not: let not the sun go down upon your wrath: neither give place to the devil.

Ephesians 4:26-27

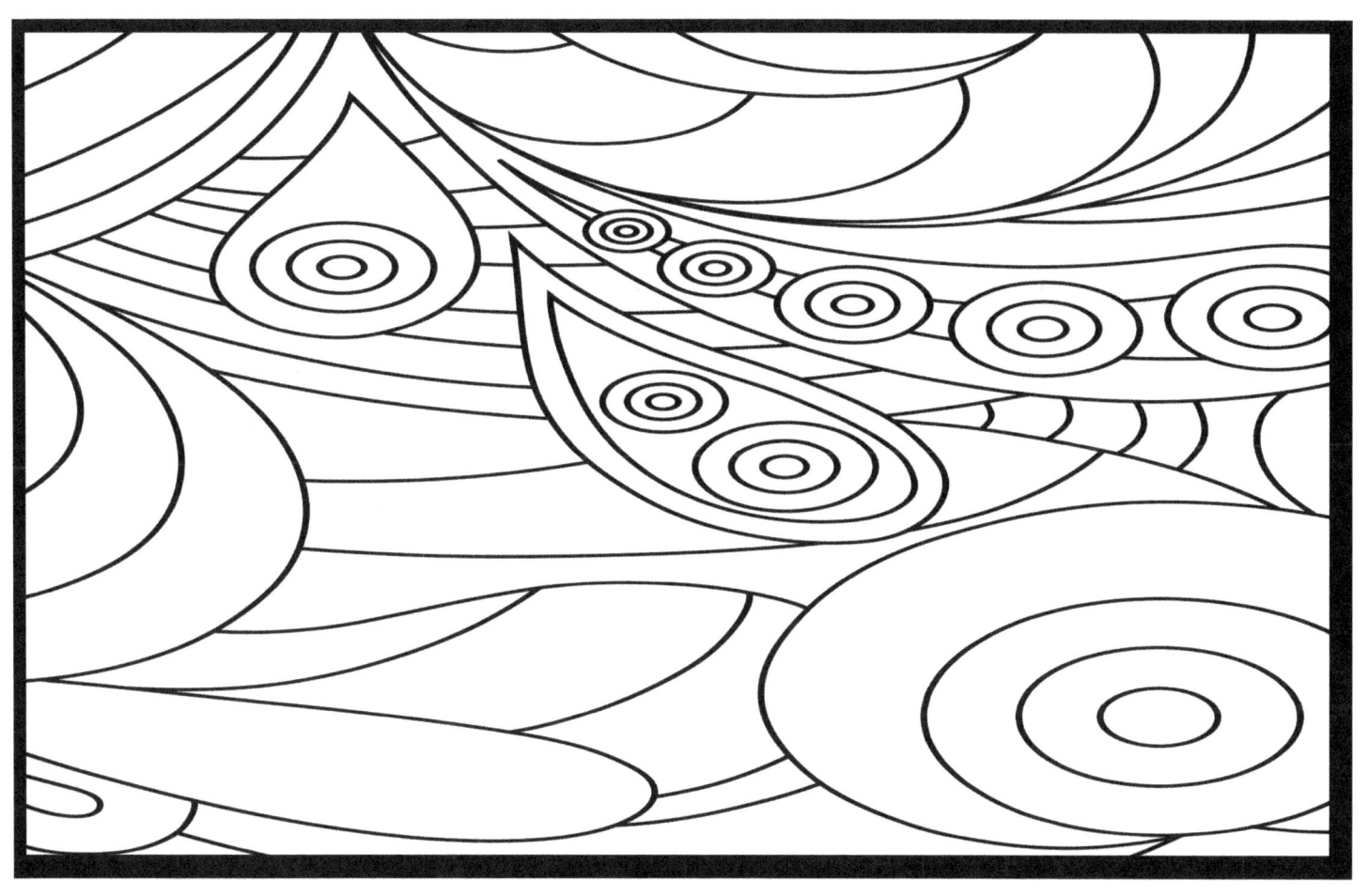

43. The pain of the past is no match for the joy of the present.

Ephesians 4:31-32

Lord, help us to color our marriage with…

_____

_____

_____

_____

_____

_____

_____

_____

_____

_____

_____

Let all bitterness, and wrath, and anger, and clamor, and evil speaking, be put away from you, with all malice: and be ye kind one to another, tender-hearted, forgiving one another, even as God for Christ's sake hath forgiven you.

Ephesians 4:31-32

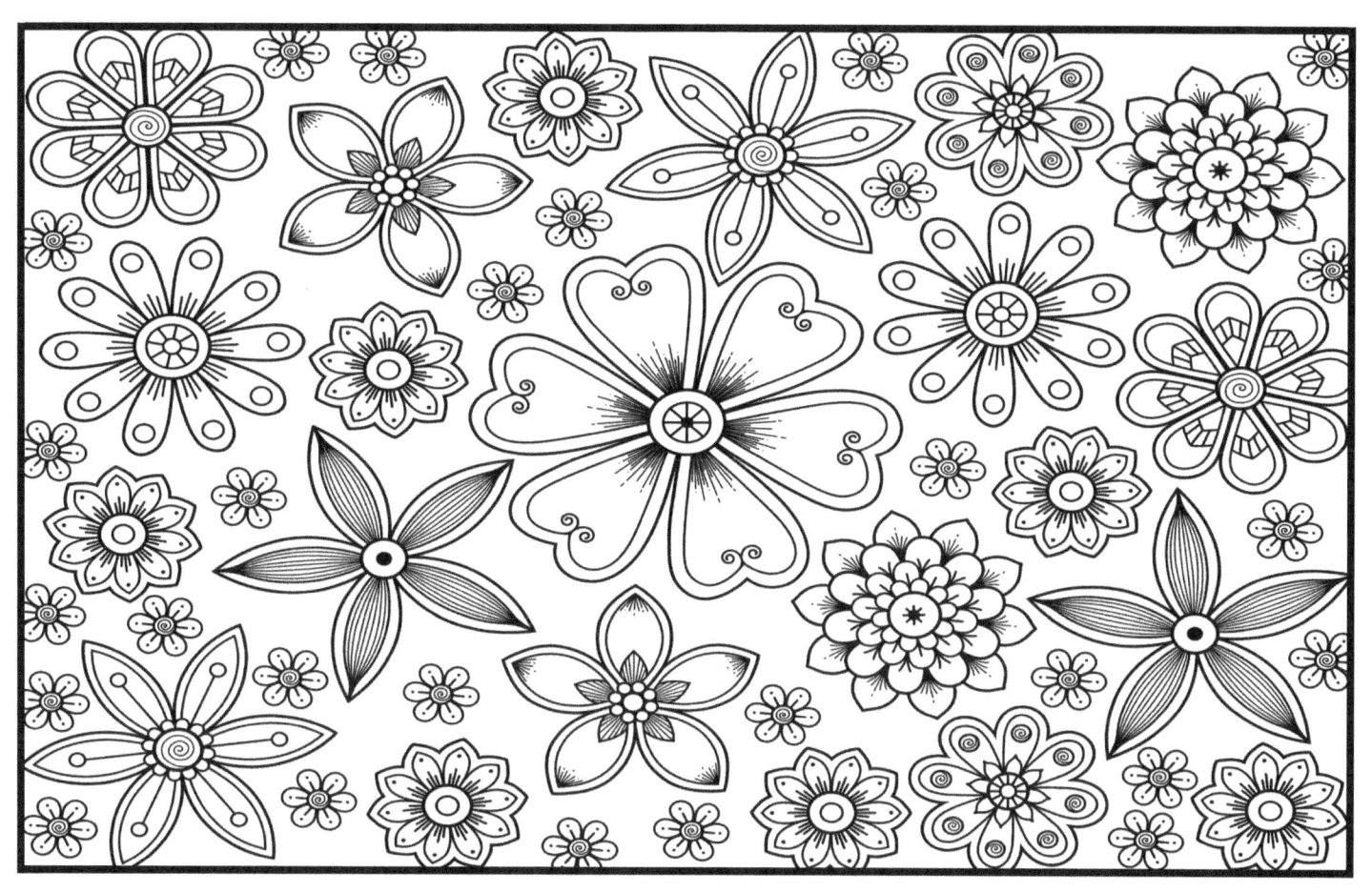

44. Be concerned about what is best for the other person.

John 15:13

Lord, help us to color our marriage with...

_____
_____
_____
_____
_____
_____
_____
_____
_____
_____
_____
_____
_____

Greater love hath no man than this,
that a man lay down his life for his friends.
John 15:13

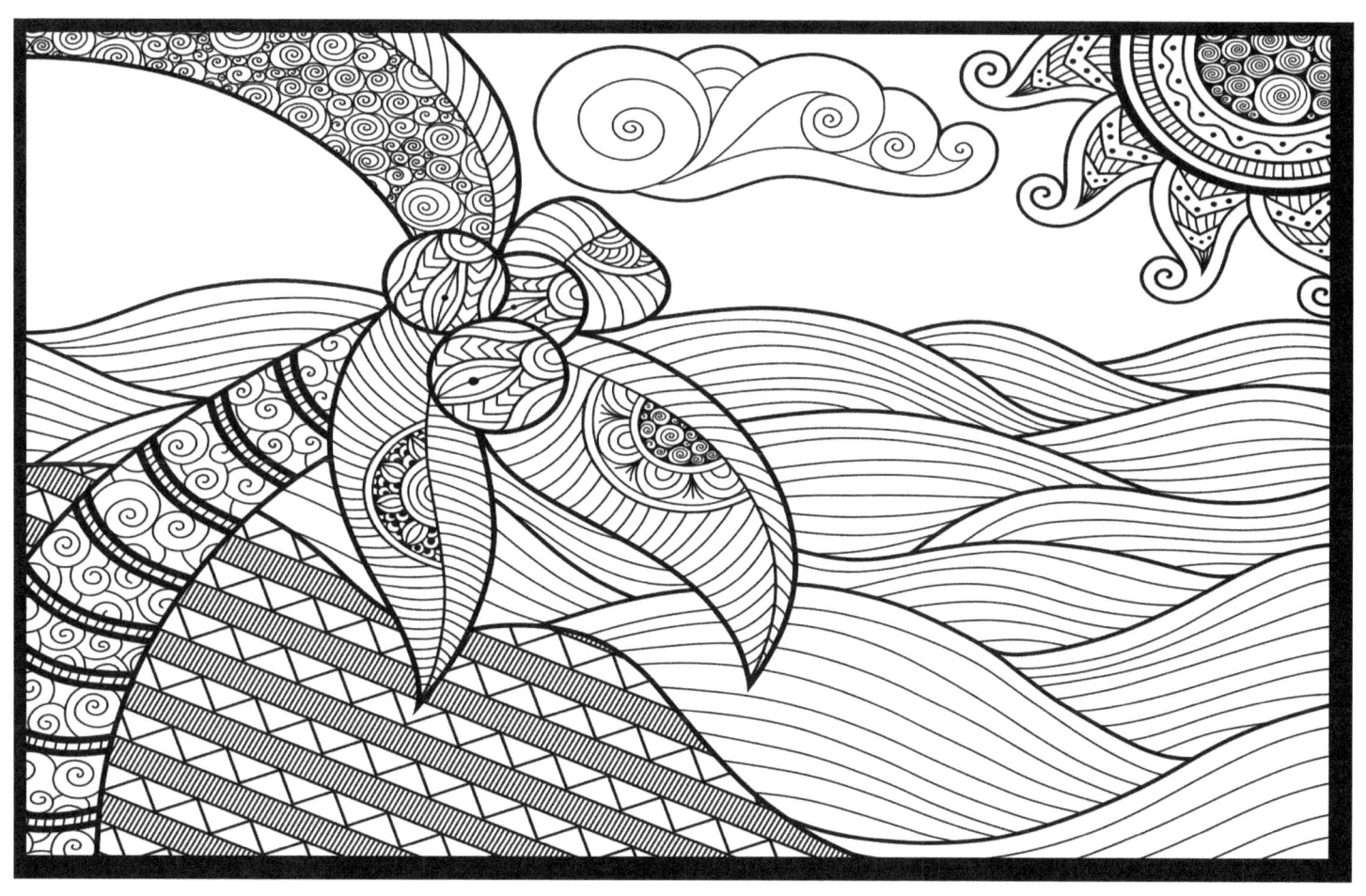

45. Trust God to lead you in the direction He has for you.

Proverbs 3:5-6

Lord, help us to color our marriage with...

_____
_____
_____
_____
_____
_____
_____
_____
_____
_____
_____

Trust in the Lord with all thine heart;
and lean not unto thine own understanding.
In all thy ways acknowledge him,
and he shall direct thy paths.
Proverbs 3:5-6

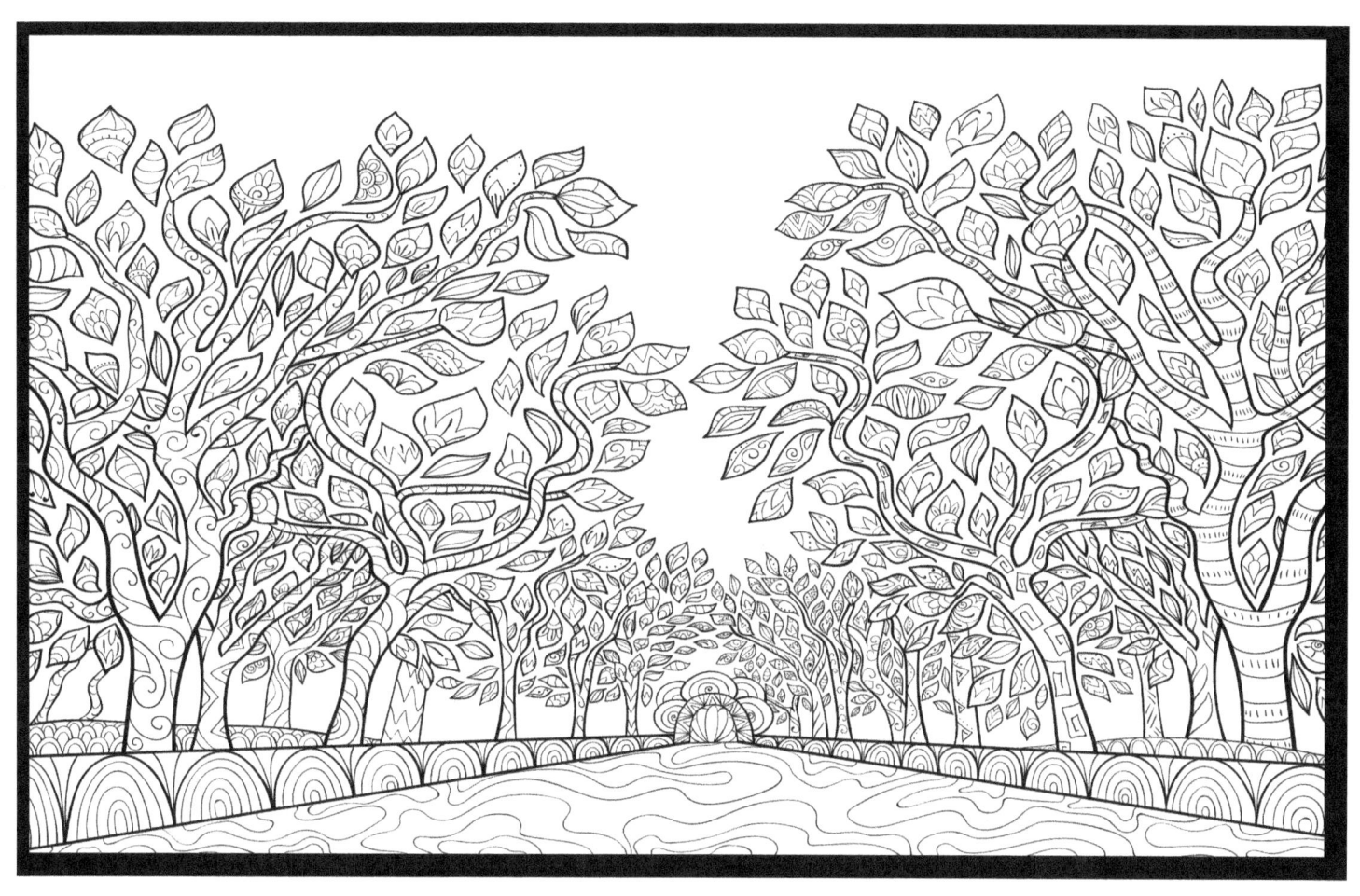

46. Go beyond the surface to find the treasure in the small things.
Matthew 13:45-46

Lord, help us to color our marriage with...

_____
_____
_____
_____
_____
_____
_____
_____
_____
_____
_____
_____
_____

Again, the kingdom of heaven is like unto a merchantman,
seeking goodly pearls: who, when he had found one pearl of
great price, went and sold all that he had, and bought it.
Matthew 13:45-46

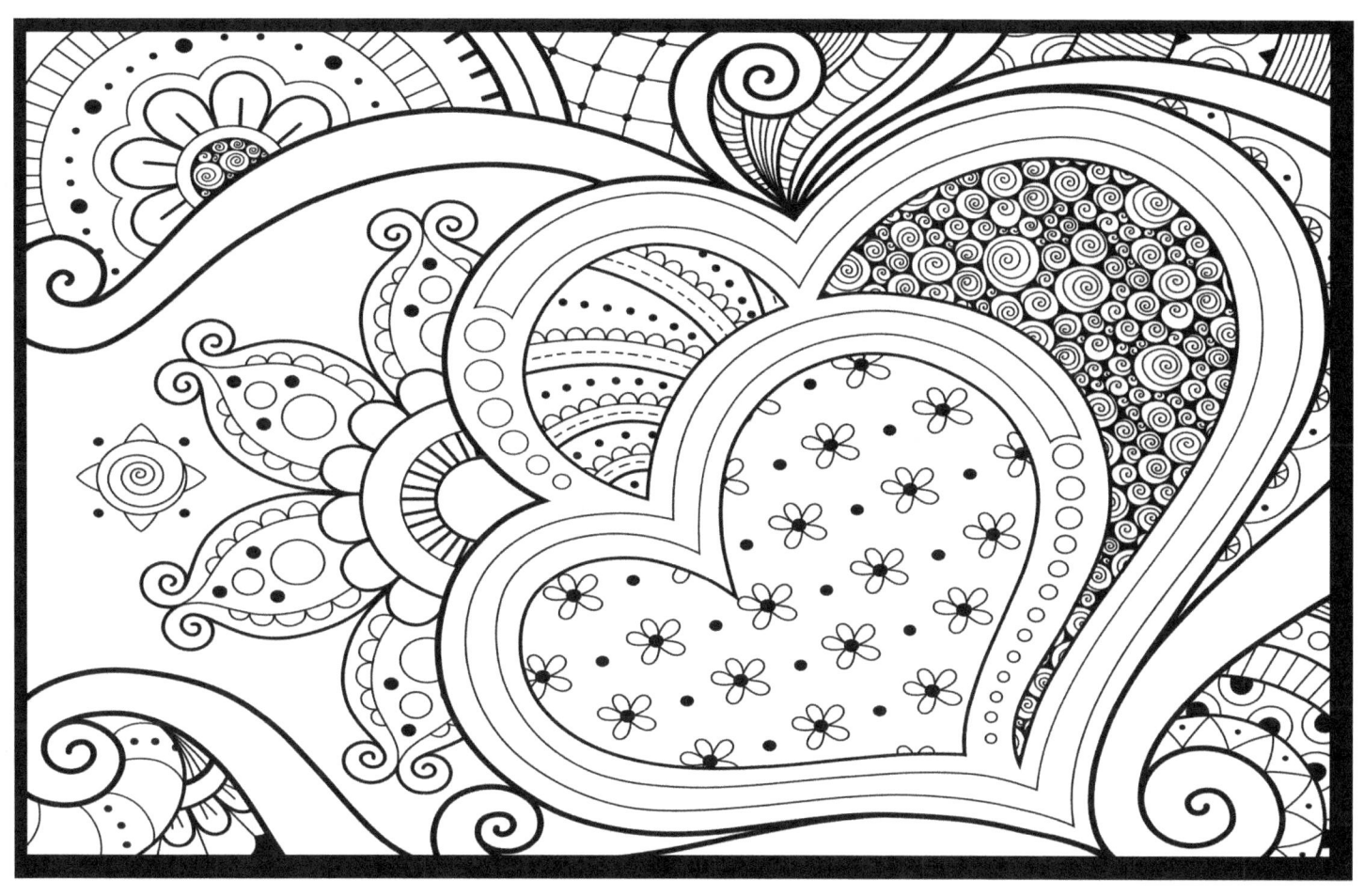

47. A seasoned word, at the right moment, can be life-changing.

Proverbs 25:11

Lord, help us to color our marriage with...

_____
_____
_____
_____
_____
_____
_____
_____
_____
_____

A word fitly spoken
is like apples of gold in pictures of silver.
Proverbs 25:11

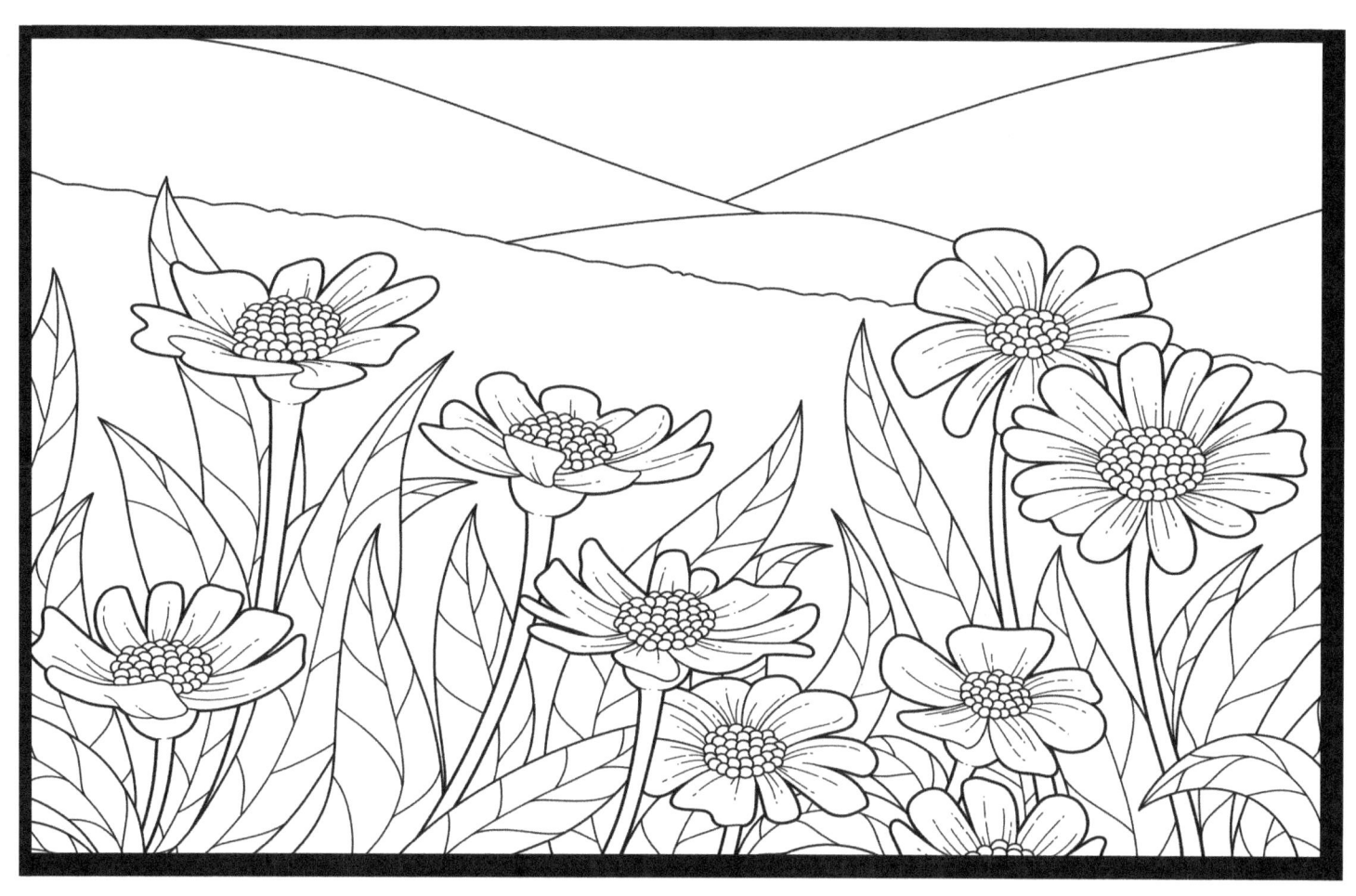

48. Rely on your faith versus facts, feelings, and fear.
John 14:27; Philippians 4:6-7

Lord, help us to color our marriage with...
_____
_____
_____
_____
_____
_____
_____
_____
_____
_____
_____

Peace I leave with you, my peace I give unto you: not as the world giveth, give I unto you. Let not your heart be troubled, neither let it be afraid.

John 14:27

Be careful for nothing; but in every thing by prayer and s upplication with thanksgiving let your requests be made known unto God. And the peace of God, which passeth all understanding, shall keep your hearts and minds through Christ Jesus.

Philippians 4:6-7

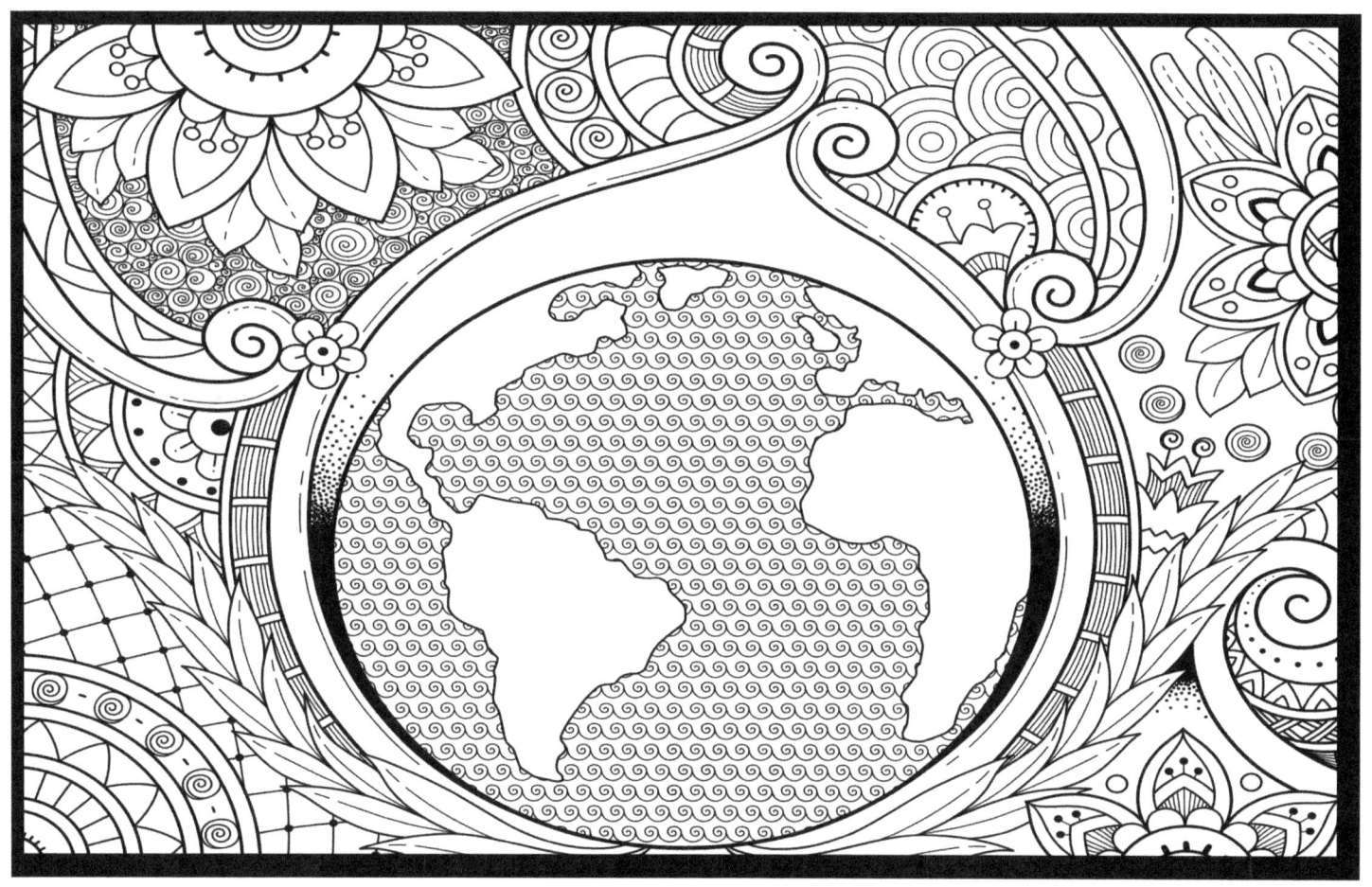

49. Avoid making major decisions in moments of emotional distress.

I Peter 5:7

Lord, help us to color our marriage with...

...casting all your care upon him; for he careth for you.

I Peter 5:7

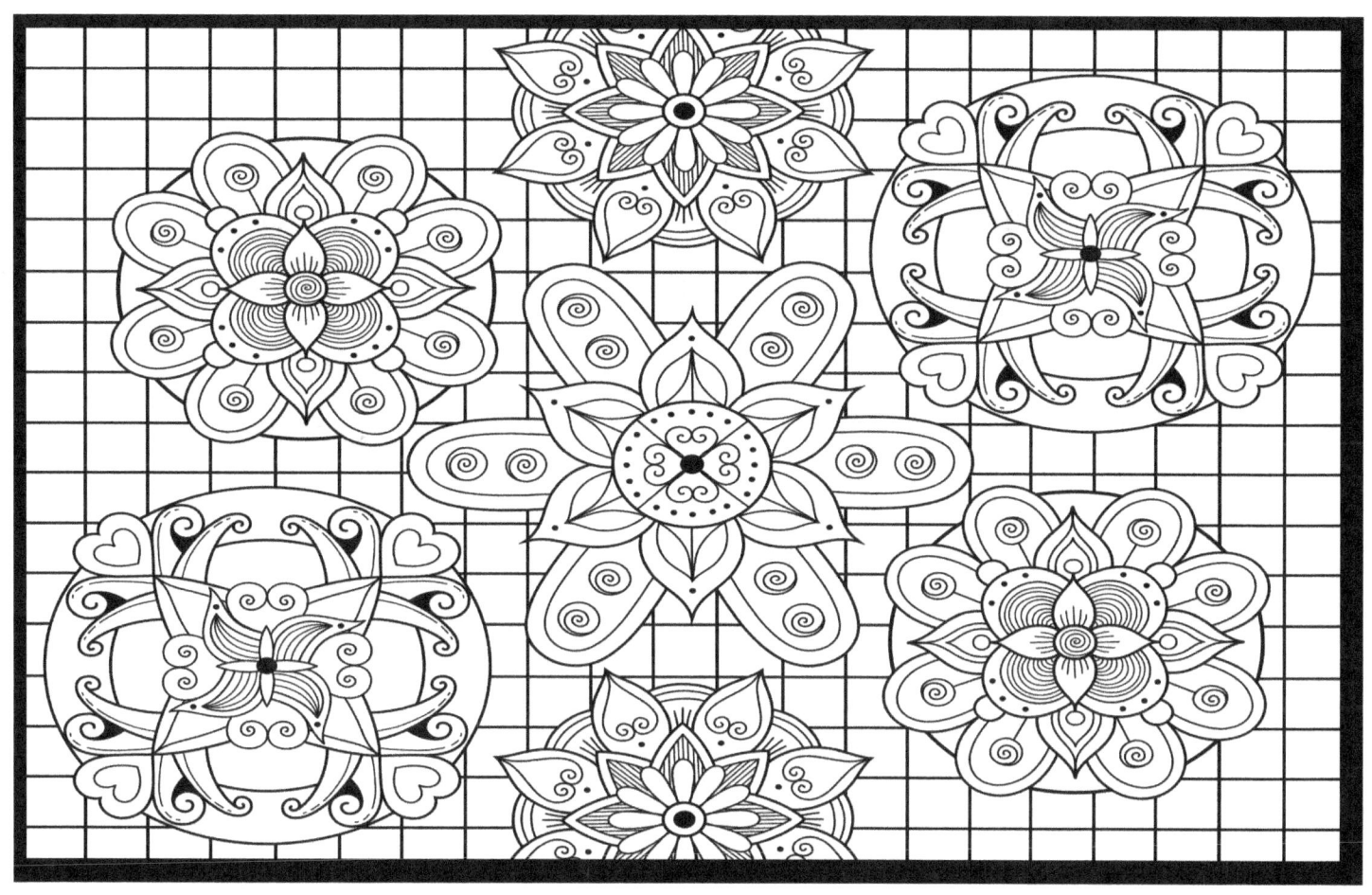

50. Both of you may experience the same situation differently.
A little understanding goes a long way.

Lord, help us to color our marriage with...

Then said his wife unto him, Dost thou still retain thine
integrity? Curse God, and die.

But he said unto her, Thou speakest as one of the
foolish women speaketh. What? Shall we receive good
at the hand of God, and shall we not receive evil?

In all this did not Job sin with his lips.

Job 2:9-10

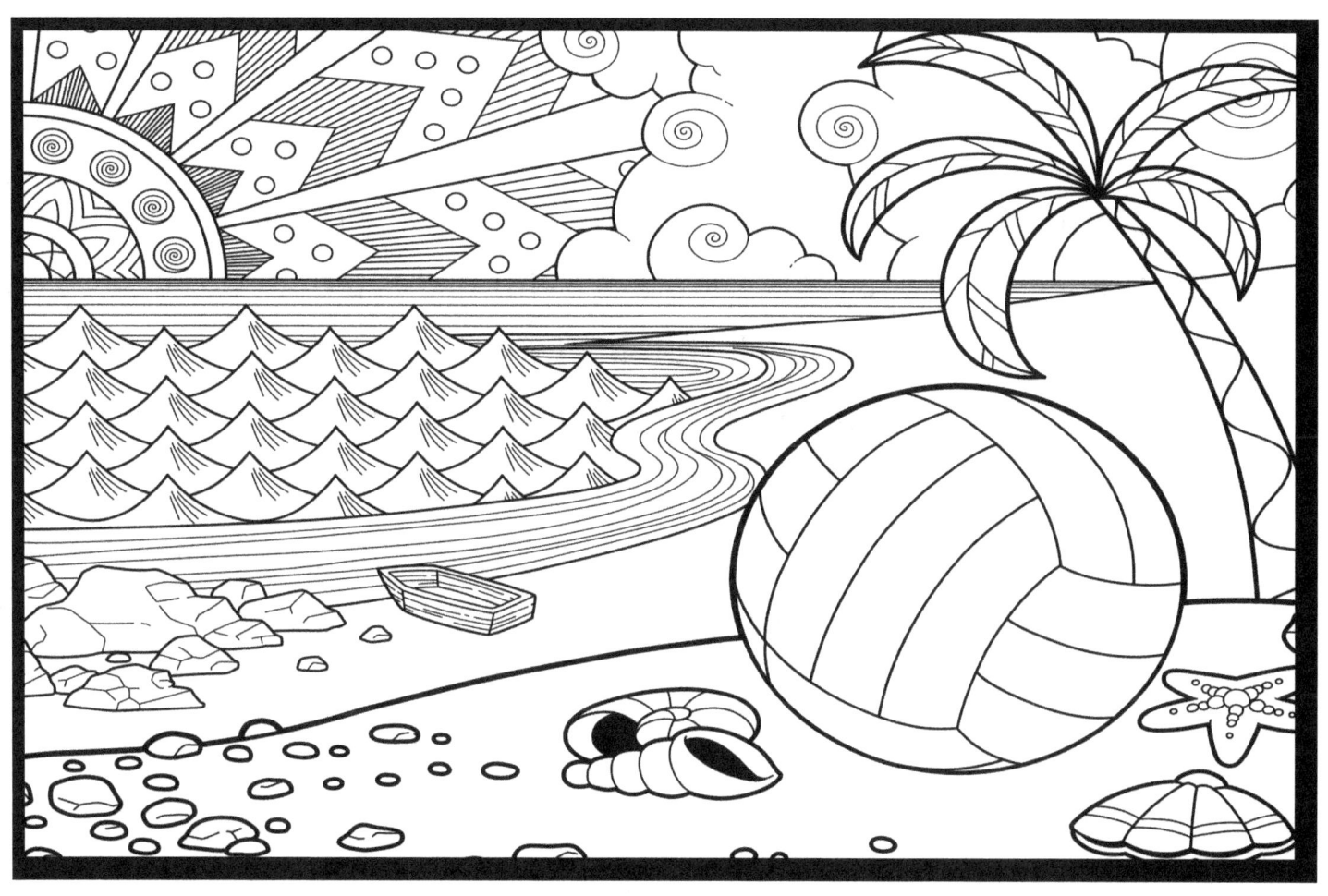

51. Success, sacrifice, and support should never be one-sided
Ecclesiastes 4:9-12

Lord, help us to color our marriage with...

_____

_____

_____

_____

_____

_____

_____

_____

_____

_____

_____

Two are better than one; because they have a good reward for their labor. For if they fall, the one will lift up his fellow: but woe to him that is alone when he falleth; for he hath not another to help him up. Again, if two lie together, then they have heat: but how can one be warm alone? And if one prevail against him, two shall withstand him; and a threefold cord is not quickly broken.

Ecclesiastes 4:9-12

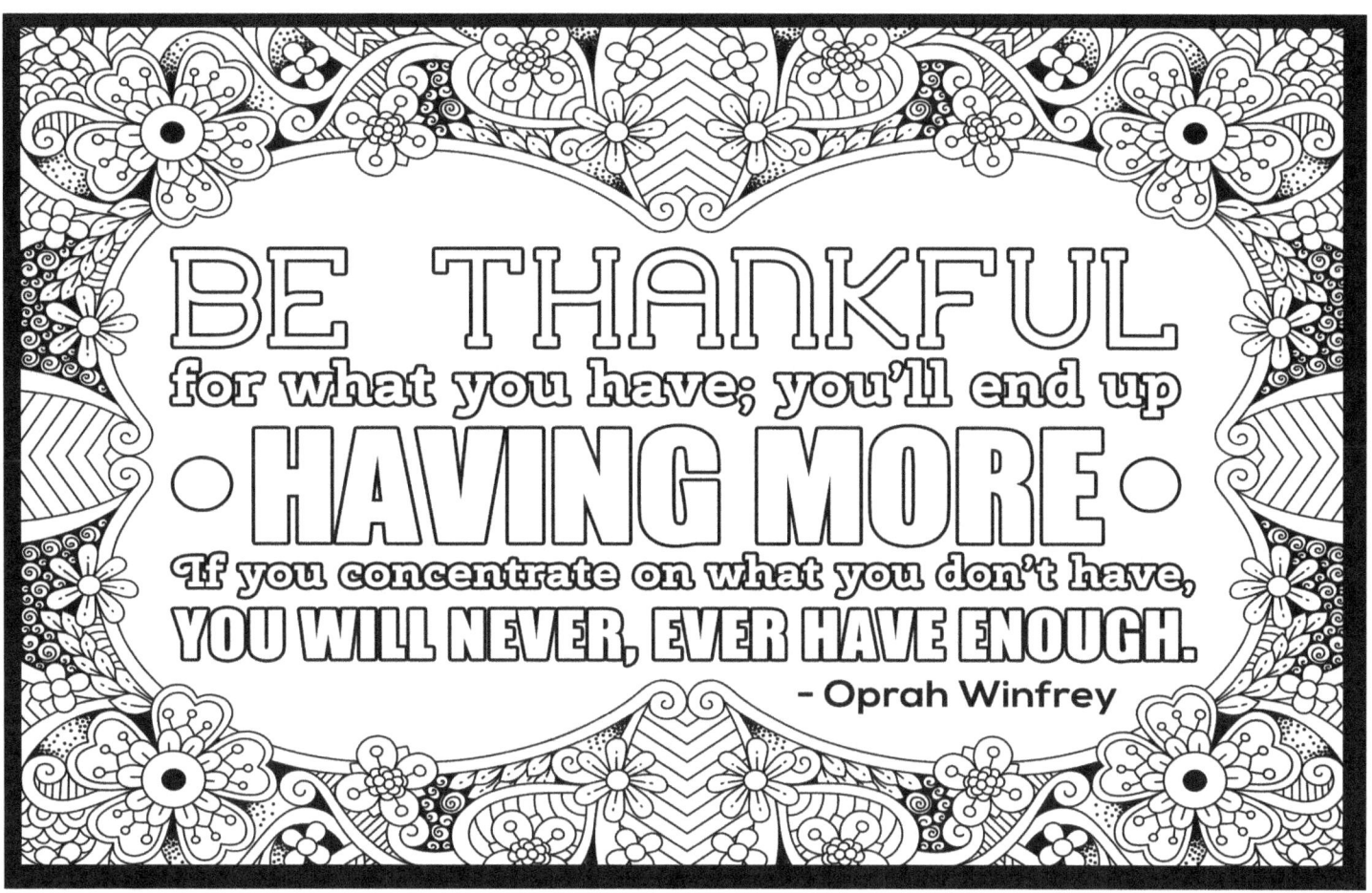

BE THANKFUL for what you have; you'll end up •HAVING MORE• If you concentrate on what you don't have, YOU WILL NEVER, EVER HAVE ENOUGH.

– Oprah Winfrey

*Create your own shade!

Lord, help us to color our marriage with...

Workshops & Coaching Events

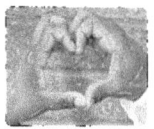 **Picture-Perfect Power Couple**
Marriage Encounter

*A two-day event designed to empower couples with creative
strategies to cultivate a satisfying and productive marriage

Dream Team – Power Couples Unite!
Discover Your Purpose
Develop Personality Synergy
Learn Your Lead Language

Picture This – The Power of a Vision-Driven Marriage
Discover Your Marital Purpose
Develop Your Marriage Vision Statement
Design Your Vision Canvas

The Art of War - Handle Conflict with P.O.I.S.E. & C.A.L.M.
Practice Communication Etiquette
Discover D.A.M. Barriers to Listening
Master the F'ing Weapons of War

Get S.H.I.F.T. Done – The Power Couple System for Success
o Develop a plan for your next Power Move
o Create S.U.P.E.R. S.M.A.R.T. Goals
o Design Your Next Level

*Ask about the virtual Picture-Perfect Marriage Encounter
www.coachlaurabrown.com